Raising
boys

Raising boys

Why boys are different – and how to help them
become happy and well-balanced men

Steve Biddulph

Illustrations by Paul Stanish

Thorsons

Thorsons
An Imprint of HarperCollins*Publishers*
77–85 Fulham Palace Road,
Hammersmith, London W6 8JB

First published in Australia by Finch Publishing Ltd, 1997
Published in the UK by Thorsons 1998

17 19 20 18 16

© Stephen Biddulph and Shaaron Biddulph, 1997

Illustrations by Paul Stanish

Steve Biddulph asserts the moral right to
be identified as the author of this work

A catalogue record for this book
is available from the British Library

ISBN 0 7225 3686 0

Printed and bound in Great Britain by
Creative Print and Design (Wales), Ebbw Vale

Publisher's Note

Notes on the text The 'Notes' section at the back of this book contains references to the text and useful additional information on specific points mentioned in the chapters. Each reference is linked by page number and relates to a particular section of the text.

Photographs The photographs in this book have been included to illustrate everyday moments in the lives of people, past and present. However, the people featured in these photographs are in no way connected with the individual stories, characters or situations presented in this book.

Photographic permissions We are grateful to the following people for their assistance in providing photographs for this book: Paul and Judi Taylor, Narelle Sonter, Jim and Jenny Smith, Elia Bastianon and Tony Wallis, Geoff and Chris Price, Glenda Downing, Chris and Tony Collins, Catherine James and Bruce Stephens, Ella and David Martin, Steve and Shaaron Biddulph, Glenys and Brian Atack, Steve and Henrietta Miller, Miles and Jane Felstead, Suzanne Jensen and Ral Lewis, Wendy Pettit and Currumbeena School, Robert and Sue Holloway, Dave Hancock and Tony James.

Acknowledgements The Author gratefully acknowledges the permission of the following for the right to reproduce copyright material in this publication: 'What Fathers Do', by Jack Kammer, is reprinted from *Full-Time Dads*, May/June 1995 issue, with the permission of the author. The segment of the article, 'Mid School Crisis', by Jane Figgis, is reproduced with the permission of the *Sydney Morning Herald*.

Steve Biddulph Part of the proceeds from Steve Biddulph's writing and lectures supports children's projects around the world, including TREATS in Hong Kong, Aboriginal Teenage Health (CAA) in Australia, Queensland Men's Helpline, Playgroups Association Australia, Parent Network in the United Kingdom, Beijing Women's Hotline in China, and AIDS prevention in South Africa.

Contents

An important note

Once, not very long ago, girl children were seen as less valuable than boys, and less able to do what boys could do.

Families would spend all their funds on getting an education for their sons, believing that education was 'wasted' on girls. A boy would be given the best food and clothing, because he was the important one in the family's future. The birth of a baby boy was seen as a blessing; a baby girl was a misfortune.

Even today, in Thailand or Nepal for instance, girls can be bought and sold, and in parts of China girl babies may be left to die. To us this seems appalling. Yet, closer to home, a long hard struggle took place to have girls valued equally and women allowed to reach their potential. This struggle still continues.

In writing a book about boys and their special needs, I wish in no way to take away from the efforts being made everywhere to advance women and girls. But it's painfully clear (to anyone who opens a newspaper) that boys are hurting too. A better world depends on making all groups happier and healthier. If we want more good men in the world, we must start treating boys with less blame and more understanding.

Steve Biddulph
Winter 1997

CHAPTER 1

What is it with boys?

Last night I drove into town for a meeting, or at least tried to, and the situation with young men was once again thrust into my face. Three cars ahead of me, the motorway was blocked. A sedan, driven by a seventeen-year-old boy, with four friends in the car, had attempted to pull out into the traffic, but failed to see a truck coming from behind. The truck had crushed the car almost in half and carried it fifty metres along the road. As I watched, seven emergency vehicles gathered: fire, rescue, police, ambulances. Men worked in teams, calmly dealing with the situation.

The young driver was gradually cut out of the wreck unconscious. His four male passengers had varying injuries. An older woman, perhaps the mother of one of the boys, came running from a nearby farm. A policeman gently comforted her.

Maleness was everywhere – inexperience and risk on the one side; competence, caring and steadiness on the other.

It kind of summed up for me the male situation. Men, when they turn out well, are wonderful. But being young and male is so vulnerable, so prone to disaster. When we see a boy born these days, we have our hearts in our mouths – how will he turn out ?

Boys at risk

Today it's the girls who are more sure of themselves, motivated, hard working. Boys are often adrift in life, failing at school, awkward in relationships, at risk for violence, alcohol and drugs, and so on. The differences start early – visit any nursery school and see for yourself. The girls work together happily; the boys 'hoon' around like Indians around a wagon train. They annoy the girls and fight with each other.

In primary school the boys' work is often sloppy and inferior. By the time they reach grade three, most boys don't read books any more. They speak in one word sentences: 'Huh?' 'Awwyeah!' In high school they don't join in with debating, concerts, councils or any non-sport activity. They pretend not to care about anything, and that 'it's cool to be a fool'.

Teenage boys are quite unsure about relationships and how to get girls to like them. Some become painfully shy, others are aggressive and unpleasant when girls are around. They seem to lack even the most basic conversation skills.

And the bottom line, of course, is safety. By fifteen years of age boys are three times more likely than girls to die from all causes combined – but especially from accidents, violence and suicide.

The good news

What we all want is young men who are happy, creative, energetic and kind. We need our boys to turn into the young men who will

care about others, and be part of the solutions of the twenty-first century. And in the meantime, we need them to do the dishes and tidy their rooms!

In the last five years a huge amount has been learned about the true nature of boys, which may surprise and delight you. We think this book will be a great relief to you to read. For thirty years it has been trendy to deny masculinity and say that boys and girls are really just the same. But as parents and teachers kept telling us, this approach wasn't working. New research is confirming parents' intuitions about boys being different in positive ways. We are beginning to understand how to *appreciate* their masculinity – in whatever form it takes – and not just squash it down.

In this book we will look at many breakthrough areas of

understanding boys. We'll explain first their *three distinct stages* of development. Then we'll examine the powerful effects of male *hormones* on boys' psychology, and how to help them ride these waves of development. We'll tell you about significant new findings about the ways in which boys' *brains* are vulnerable, and how to help them develop better communication skills. Then some stories and ideas about the important relationship between *mothers* and sons, the vital place of *fathers*, and how *schools* can be dramatically improved. We'll examine *sport*, which has become a real hazard – though it could be so good for boys. We'll talk about boys and *sex*. And lastly, some ways in which the whole *community* can support boys turning into men.

Boys can be just great. We can make them so. Understanding is the key.

The three stages of boyhood

Boys don't just grow up in a smooth and even way. You can't just shovel in cereal, provide clean T-shirts, and have them one day wake up as a man! A certain sequence has to be followed. Anyone who spends time around boys will be amazed at how they change, and the range of moods and energies which they show at different times. The puzzle is to understand what is needed – and when.

Luckily, boys have been around for a very long time, and we are not the first to deal with them. Every culture in the world has encountered the challenge of raising boys, and has come up with solutions. It's only in recent decades, which have been so swept with change, that we have failed to adopt a real plan of action for raising boys well. We've just been too busy doing other things!

The three stages of boyhood are timeless and universal. Whenever I talk about them with parents, they say, 'That's right!', because the stages match their experience.

The three stages at a glance

1   The first stage is from ***birth to six*** – the age when the boy primarily belongs to his mother. He is 'her' boy, even though his father may play a very large role. The aim at this age is to give strong love and security, and to 'switch a boy on' to life as a warm and welcoming experience.

2   The second stage – from ***six to fourteen*** – when the boy, out of his own internal drives, starts wanting to learn to be a man, and looks more and more to his father for interest and activity. (Though his mother remains very involved, and the wider world is beckoning too.) The purpose of this stage is to build competence and skill while developing kindness and playfulness too – becoming a balanced person. This is when a boy becomes happy and secure about being male.

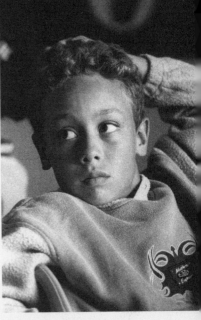

3 Finally, the years from *fourteen to adult* – when the boy needs input from male mentors if he is to complete the journey into being fully grown-up. Mum and dad step back a little, but they must organise some good mentors in their son's life or he will have to rely on an ill-equipped peer group for his sense of self. The aim is to learn skills, responsibility and self-respect by joining more and more with the adult community.

Please note: These stages do not indicate a sudden or sharp shift from one parent to another. The best situation is one where both parents are very involved right through childhood and adolescence. The stages indicate a shift of emphasis: that the father 'comes to the fore' more from six to thirteen, and the importance of mentors increases from fourteen onwards. Mentors should always be vetted by parents for safety and integrity.

The three stages tell us a lot about what to do. For example, it's clear that fathers of boys from six to fourteen must not be just busy workaholics, or absent themselves emotionally or physically from the family. If they do, then this will certainly damage their boys. (Yet most fathers this century have done just that – as many of us can remember from our own childhoods.)

The stages tell us that we need to bring in extra help from the community when our sons are in their mid-teens – the role that used to be taken by family members (uncles and grandfathers) or the tradesman–apprentice relationship. Too often, teenagers move outwards into the big world but no-one is there to catch them, and they spend their teens and early adulthood in a dangerous half-way stage. Some just never grow up at all.

It's a fair bet that many problems – especially with boys' behaviour, poor school motivation, and with young men getting into strife with the law (drink-driving, fighting, etc.) – are because we haven't known about these stages and haven't provided the right human ingredients at the right times.

The stages are so important that we must look at them in more detail and decide how to respond. That's what we'll do now.

From birth to six: the gentle years

Babies are babies. Being a boy or girl is not a concern to them, and needn't be to us either. Babies love to be cuddled, to play, to be tickled and to giggle; to explore and be swooshed around. Their personalities vary a lot. Some are easy to handle – quiet and relaxed, and sleep long hours. Others are noisy and wakeful, always wanting some action. Some are anxious and fretful, needing lots of reassurance that we are there, and that we love them.

What babies and toddlers need most is to form a special bond with at least one person. Usually this person is their mother. Partly because she is the one who is most willing and motivated, partly because she provides the milk and partly because she tends to be cuddly, restful and soothing in her approach, a mother is usually the best equipped to provide what a baby needs. Her own hormones (especially prolactin – released into her bloodstream as she breastfeeds) prime her to want to be with her child and to give it her full attention.

Except for breastfeeding, dads can provide all a baby needs but tend to do it differently. Studies show them to be more vigorous in their playing, they like to stir children up, while mothers like to calm them down. (Though if fathers get as deprived of sleep as mothers sometimes do, they too would want to calm them down!)

Gender differences begin to show

Some gender differences between boys and girls do begin to appear early on. Boy babies are less sensitive to faces. Girl babies have a much better sense of touch. Boys grow faster and stronger, yet they are more troubled by separations from their mother. By toddlerhood, when boys play they move around more and occupy more space. They like to handle and manipulate objects more – and build high buildings out of blocks, while girls prefer low-rise. At nursery school boys tend to ignore a new child who arrives in the group, while girls will notice them and befriend them.

And sadly, adults tend to treat boys more harshly. Studies have shown that parents hug and cuddle girl children far more, even as newborn babies. They tend to talk less to boy babies. And mothers of boys are likely to hit them harder and more often than they do girl children.

If a mother is the main care-giver, a boy will see her as his first model for intimacy and love. From toddlerhood on, if she sets limits with her son firmly, but without hitting or shaming him, he will take this in his stride. He knows he has a special place in her heart.

Her interest and fun in teaching and talking to him helps his brain to develop

more verbal skills, and makes him more sociable. We'll see later that this is important for boys, because they need more help than girls to 'catch on' to social skills.

If a mother is terribly depressed and therefore unresponsive in the first year or two of her son's life, his brain may undergo changes to become a 'sad brain'. If she is angry, hitting or hurting him, he will be confused over whether she loves him. A mother needs others to support her, so that she can relax and do this important work. She needs to be cared for, so that she can care for her baby.

A mother shows delight when her child catches frogs or makes mud pies, and admires his achievements. His father tickles him and play-wrestles with him, and is also gentle and nurturing, reading stories and comforting him when he is sick. The little boy learns that men are kind, as well as exciting; that men read books, and are capable in the home.

Early childcare is not good for boys

If at all possible, a boy should stay home with one of his parents until age three. Childcare of the institutional kind – creches or childcare centres – does not suit boys' nature under this age. Many studies have shown that boys are more prone than girls to separation anxiety and to becoming emotionally shut down as a result of feeling abandoned. Also a boy of this age can develop restless or aggressive behaviour in childcare and carry this label, and the role that goes with it, right on into school.

Care by a loving relative, or family daycare with a loving carer, is far better than a creche situation for toddlers under three. Children under three need to spend the long days of childhood with people to whom they are very special. The first lessons boys need to learn are in closeness, trust, warmth, fun and kindness.

In short

Under six years of age, gender isn't a big deal, and it shouldn't be made so. Mothers are usually the primary parent, but a father can take this place. What matters is that one or two key people love this child and make him central for these few years. That way, he develops inner security for life, and his brain acquires the skills of intimate communication and a love of learning and interaction.

These years are soon over. Enjoy your little boy while you can!

From six to thirteen: learning to be male

At around six years of age, a big change takes place in boys. There seems to be a sudden 'switching on' of boys' masculinity at this age. Even boys who have not watched much TV suddenly want to play with swords, wear Superman capes, fight and wrestle, and make lots of noise. Something else happens that is really important: it's been observed in all societies around the world. At around six years of age, little boys seem to 'lock on' to their dad, or stepdad, or whichever male is around and want to be with him, learn from him and copy him. They want to 'study how to be male'.

YA HOLD YA
ARMS LIKE
THIS!

If a dad ignores his son at this time, the boy will often launch an all-out campaign to get his attention. Once I consulted in the case of a little boy who became seriously ill for no apparent reason. He was placed in intensive care. His father, a leading medical specialist, flew back from a conference in America to be with him, and the boy got better. The father went away to another conference, and the illness came back. We asked the father to reconsider his lifestyle which involved being on the road for *eight months a year*! He did this, and the boy has not been ill since.

Boys may steal, wet the bed, act aggressively at school and develop any number of problem behaviours just to get Dad to take an interest.

Mums still matter just as much

This sudden shift of interest to the father does not mean that Mum leaves the picture. In some countries (such as the United States) mothers often distance themselves from their boys at this age, to 'toughen them up'. (This was also the age that the upper classes here in Britain sent their boys to boarding school.) But as Olga Silverstein has argued in her book *The Courage to Raise Good*

Men, this is a dumb idea. Boys need to know they can count on Mum, and don't have to shut off their tender feelings. Things work best if they can stay close to Mum, but add Dad too. If a dad feels a child is too taken up with his mother's world (which can happen) then he should increase his own involvement – not criticise the mother! Perhaps he is too critical or expects too much, and the boy is afraid of him.

If, in the early years, a mother suddenly withdraws her presence or her warmth and affection, then a terrible thing happens: the boy, to control his grief and pain, shuts down the part of him that connects with her – his tender and loving part. He finds it is just too painful to feel loving feelings if they are no longer reciprocated by his mother. If a boy shuts down this part of him, he will have trouble as an adult expressing warmth or tenderness to his own partner or children, and be a rather tense and brittle man. We all know men like this (bosses, fathers, even husbands) who are emotionally restricted and awkward with people. We can make sure our sons are not like this by hugging them whether they are five, ten or fifteen.

FIVE FATHERING ESSENTIALS

Here are some more basic ingredients for fathering:

- *Start early*. Be involved in the pregnancy – talk about your hopes for the child, be at the birth. Get involved in baby care right from the start. This is the key time for relationship building. Caring for a baby 'primes' you hormonally and alters your life priorities. So beware! Fathers who care for babies physically start to get fascinated and very in tune with them – it's called 'engrossment'. Men can become the expert at getting babies back to sleep in the middle of the night – walking them, bouncing, singing gently, or whatever works for you! Don't settle for being a klutz around babies – keep at it, get support and advice from the baby's mother and other experienced friends. And take pride in your ability.

  Even if you have a demanding career, use your weekends or holidays to get immersed in your child. From the age of two onwards, invite your partner to go away for the weekend and leave you and the toddler alone – so you know you are capable.

- *Make time.* This is the bottom line. Listen closely – for fathers this is the most important sentence in this whole book: *If you routinely work a fifty-five or sixty-hour week, including travel times, you just won't cut it as a dad.* Your sons will have problems in life, and it will be down to you. Fathers need to get home in time to play, laugh, teach and tickle their children. Corporate life and also small business can be enemies of the family. Often fathers find that the answer is to accept a lower income and be around their families more. Next time you're offered a 'promotion' involving longer hours and more nights away from home, seriously consider telling your boss 'Sorry, my kids come first'.

- *Be demonstrative.* Hugging, holding and playing tickling and wrestling games can take place right through to adulthood! And do gentler things too – kids respond to quiet storytelling, sitting together, singing or playing music. Tell your kids how great, beautiful, creative and intelligent they are (often, and with feeling). If your parents were not demonstrative, you will just have to learn.

Some men fear that cuddling their son will make him a 'sissy' (for which you can read 'gay'). It won't. In fact, the opposite may be true. Many gay or bisexual men I have spoken to say that a lack of fatherly affection was part of what made male affection more important to them.

- **Lighten up.** Enjoy your kids. Being with them out of guilt or obligation is second-rate, and (in any case) 'quality time' is a myth. Experiment to find those activities that you both enjoy. Take the 'pressure to achieve' off your kids – but insist that they contribute in the home. Limit them to one or at most two sports or activities, so they have time to just 'be'. Release that 'racing around' time, and devote it instead to walks, games and conversations. Avoid over-competitiveness in any activity beyond what is good fun. Teach your kids, continuously, everything you know.

- **Heavy down.** Some fathers today are lightweight 'good-time' dads who leave all the hard stuff to their partners. Get involved in the decisions, supervise homework and housework. Develop ways of discipline which are calm but definite. Don't hit – although with young children you may have to hold and restrain them from time to time. Insist on respect. Don't just be one of the kids. Do listen to them and take their feelings into account. Talk with your partner about the big picture: 'How are we going overall? What changes are needed?' Parenting as a team can add a new bond between you and your partner.

WHEN BOYS ARE SHORT

Parents sometimes worry if their son is not growing as tall as other boys. Indications are that this worry is needless. A recent study of 180 boys and 78 girls, aged eight to fourteen, who were sufficiently short to be referred to a special centre for assessment, found that short children are no more likely to be maladjusted than taller children.

Earlier research suggested shorter youngsters were more likely to be shy, anxious or depressed, but this latest study has not found this to be so. It may be that society is changing, and is more diverse and tolerant. If a child is praised and valued, and has good communication within the family, then being different will cause much less stress.

In the study, short boys described themselves as less socially active but did not have more behaviour problems than boys of average height. Girls in the study often had even better mental health than girls of normal height. Children whose parents were short themselves seemed to have far fewer problems, probably because of the good role-modelling being provided by their parents. These parents were less likely to be worried or seek medical help for shortness.

In the United States 20,000 children have taken human growth hormone to overcome shortness, a treatment costing around $30,000. Doctors only recommend the hormone treatment if it is medically necessary, such as when kidney failure or other condtions have caused a deficiency in the growth hormone. Paediatricians do not believe that psychological reasons are sufficient to justify the treatment, which is painful and inconvenient, and 'can do more harm than good'.

In our world today, it's high time we welcomed a wider range of sizes and shapes in adults and children.

Finding a man to be like

The six- to fourteen-year-old boy still adores his mother and has plenty to learn from her. But his interests are changing – he is becoming more focused on what men have to offer. A boy knows that he is turning into a man. He has to 'download the software' from an available male to complete his development.

The mother's job is to relax about this, and stay warm and supportive. The father's job is to progressively step up his involvement. If there is no father around, then the child depends more on finding other men – at school for instance. Yet men are disappearing from the teaching profession, especially in primary schools, which creates a problem. (More on this later.)

A single mother

For thousands of years single mothers have needed to raise boys without a man in the house. There's no doubt that women can raise good men, but – and it's a big but – the ones I have spoken to who succeeded always stress that they found good male role-models, calling in help from uncles, good friends, schoolteachers, sports coaches, youth leaders and so on (choosing with great care to guard against the risk of sexual abuse). They emphasise, too, that they needed lots of extra support (friendship, massage, self-time) in order to cope. (For more on this topic see page 97.)

IS IT ADD OR DDD (Dad Deficit Disorder)?

Two years ago, a man called Don came up to me after a lecture, and told me this story. Don was a truck driver and, a year earlier, his son, aged eight, had been diagnosed with Attention Deficit Disorder. Don read the diagnosis and, for want of better information, decided it meant his son Troy wasn't getting enough attention. That, surely, was what 'attention deficit' meant!

Don set himself the goal of getting more involved with Troy. He had always taken the view that raising children was best left to the 'Missus' while he worked to pay the bills. Now all of that changed. In the holidays, and after school when possible, Troy rode in the truck with his dad. On weekends, whereas Don had often spent the time away with mates who collected and rode classic motorcycles, Troy now came along too.

'We had to tone down the language and clean up our act a bit, but the blokes all understood, and some started bringing their kids too,' Don told me with a smile.

The good news: Troy calmed down so much in a couple of months that he came off his Ritalin medication – he wasn't 'ADD' any longer. But father and son continue to hang out together – because they enjoy it. Note: We are not saying here that all instances of Attention Deficit Disorder are really dad-deficit disorders – but quite a lot are. (For more about ADD and boys, see page 172.)

In short

All through the primary school years and into secondary school, boys should spend a lot of time with their fathers and mothers, gaining their help, learning how to do things, and enjoying their company. From an emotional viewpoint, the father is now more significant. The boy is ready to learn from his dad, and listens to what he has to say. Often he will take more notice of his father. It's enough to drive a mother wild!

This window of time – from about age six to the fourteenth birthday – is the major opportunity for a father to have an influence on (and build the foundations of masculinity in) his son. Now is the time to 'make time'. Little things count: playing in the backyard on summer evenings; going for walks and yarning about life and telling him about your own childhood; working on hobbies or sports together for the enjoyment of doing it. This is when good memories are laid down that will nourish your son, and you, for decades to come.

Don't be deterred if your son acts 'cool', as he has learned to do this from his schoolmates. Persist and you will find a laughing, playful boy just under the surface. Enjoy this time when he really is wanting to be with you. By mid-adolescence his interests will pull him more and more into a wider world beyond. All I can do here is plead with you – don't leave it too late!

Fourteen and onwards: becoming a man

At around fourteen years of age a new stage begins. Usually by now the boy is growing fast, and a remarkable thing is happening on the inside – his testosterone levels have increased by almost 800 percent!

Although every boy is different, it's common for boys at this age to get a little argumentative, restless and moody. It's not that they are turning bad – just that they are being born into a new self, and birth always involves some struggle. They are needing to find answers to big questions, to begin new adventures and challenges, and to learn competencies for living – and their body clock is urging them on.

SON, I'VE FIXED THE TRAIN SET !

I believe this is the age when we fail kids the most. In our society all we offer the mid-teens is 'more of the same': more school, more of the routines of home. But the adolescent is hungry for something more. He is hormonally and physically ready to break out into an adult role, but we want him to wait another five or six years! It's little wonder that problems arise.

What's needed is something that will engage the spirit of a boy – pull him headlong into some creative effort or passion that gives his life wings. All the things that parents have nightmares about (adolescent risk-taking, alcohol, drugs and criminal activity) happen because we do not find channels for young men's desire for glory and heroic roles. Boys look out at the larger society and see little to believe in or join in with. Even their rebellion is packaged up and sold back to them by advertisers and the music industry.

They want to jump somewhere better and higher, but that place is nowhere in sight.

What old societies did

In every society before ours – from Eskimo to African – in every time and place that has been studied, the mid-teen boys received a burst of intensive care and attention from the whole community. These cultures knew something we are still learning – that *parents cannot raise teenage boys without getting the help of other adults* who are trustworthy and willing to be involved long-term.

One reason for this is that fourteen-year-old sons and their fathers drive each other crazy. Often it's all a father can manage to love his son. Trying to do this *and* teach him can be just impossible. (Remember your dad teaching you to drive?) Somehow the two males just get their horns tangled and make each other worse. If someone else can supplement, then dads and sons can relax a little. (Some wonderful movies have been based on this – for instance, *Searching for Bobby Fisher* and *The Run of the Country* starring Albert Finney.)

Traditionally, two things were done to help young men into adulthood. First, they were 'taken on' and *mentored* into adulthood by one or more men who cared about them and taught them important skills for living. And second, at certain stages of this mentoring process, the young men were taken away by the community of older men and *initiated.* This meant being put through some serious growing-up processes, including testing, sacred teaching and new responsibilities.

A LAKOTA INITIATION

The Native American people known as the Lakota may be familiar to you from the movie *Dances with Wolves*. They were a vigorous and successful society, with a rich culture, characterised by especially good relationships between men and women.

At around the age of fourteen Lakota boys were sent on a 'vision quest' or initiation test. This involved sitting and fasting on a mountain peak to await a vision or hallucination brought on by hunger. This vision would include a being who would carry messages from the spirit world to guide the boy's life. As the boy fasted, and trembled alone on the peak, he would hear mountain lions snarl and move in the darkness below him. In fact the sounds were made by the men of the tribe, keeping watch, to ensure the boy's safety. A young person was too precious to the Lakota to endanger needlessly.

Eventually when the young man returned to the tribe, his achievement was celebrated. But from that day, for two whole years, *he was not permitted to speak directly to his mother*.

Lakota mothers, like the women of all hunter-gatherer groups, are very close and affectionate with their children, and the children often sleep alongside them in the women's huts and tents. The Lakota believed that if the boy spoke to his mother immediately following his entry into manhood, the attraction back into boyhood would be so great that he would 'fall' back into the world of women and never grow up.

After the two years had passed, a ceremonial rejoining of the mother and son took place, but by this time he was a man and able to relate to her as such. Women who have heard me tell this story in gatherings have often found it very moving – it brings both grief and joy. The reward that Lakota mothers gained from this 'letting go' is that they were assured their sons would return as respectful and close adult friends.

We can contrast the Lakota experience with modern-day sons and their mothers, who (according to writers like Babette Smith in *Mothers and Sons*) often remain in an awkward, distant or rather infantile relationship for life. Their sons fear getting close and yet, being uninitiated as men, they never really escape. Instead, they relate to all women in a dependent and immature way. Not having entered the community of men, they are distrustful of other men and have few real friends. They are afraid of commitment to women because for them it means being mothered, and that means being controlled. They are real 'nowhere men'.

It's only by leaving the world of women that young men can break the mother-mould and relate to women as fellow adults. Domestic violence, unfaithfulness and the inability to make a marriage work may all result not from any problem with women but from men's failure to take boys on this transforming journey.

You might think that (in the old societies) the boys' mothers, and perhaps the fathers too, would resent or fear their son being taken over by others. But this was not the case. The initiators were men they had known and trusted all their lives. The women understood and welcomed this help, because they sensed the need for it. They were giving up a rather troublesome boy, and

OVERCOMING BOYS' TENDENCY TO ARROGANCE

It's possible that boys are naturally prone to a certain degree of arrogance. Until recently, boys were often raised expecting to be waited on by women. In some cultures, boys are still treated like little gods. In today's world the result can be an obnoxious boy that no-one wants to be around.

It's therefore very important that boys are taught humbleness – through experiences such as having to apologise, having to do work to help others and always having to be respectful to others. Kids have to know their place in the world, or the world will most likely teach them a harsh lesson.

Whenever you are treated badly by youngsters – jostled in the street by a skateboarder, treated rudely by a young salesperson or have your house burgled, you are dealing with youngsters who have not been properly humbled.

Teenagers are naturally prone to be somewhat self-absorbed, to fit their morality to their own self interest and to be thoughtless of others. Our job as parents is to engage them in vigorous discussions about their obligations to others, fairness, and plain right and wrong. We must reinforce some basics – 'Be responsible. Think things through. Consider others. Think of consequences'. Just loving your kids isn't enough, some toughness is necessary. Mothers begin this, fathers reinforce it and elders add their weight if it still hasn't sunk in.

One good strategy is to have boys involved in service to others – elderly, disabled, or young children whom they help or teach. They learn the satisfaction of service and grow in self-worth at the same time.

getting back a more mature and integrated young man. And they were probably very proud of him.

The initiation into adulthood was not a one-off 'weekend special'. It could involve months of teaching about how to behave as a man, what responsibilities they were taking on, and where to find strength and direction. The ceremonies we normally hear about were only the marker events. Sometimes these ceremonies were cruel and frightening (and we would not want to return to these) but they were done with purpose and care, and were spoken of with great appreciation by those who had passed through them.

To sum up: traditional societies depended for their survival on raising competent and responsible young men. It was a life-and-death issue, and never left to chance. They developed very proactive programmes for doing this. And the process involved the whole adult community in a concerted effort. (Some ways we might go about this, appropriate to our times, are described in the final chapter, 'A community challenge'.)

In the modern world

Mentoring today is mostly unplanned and piecemeal, and lots of young men don't receive any mentoring at all. Those doing the

BEWARE OF GOOD LOOKIN' SHEILAS — DON'T OVERTIGHTEN WITH THAT WRENCH — BUY LAND, SON — THEY'RE NOT MAKING ANY MORE, HEH, HEH, HEH.

THE STORY OF NAT, STAN AND THE MOTORBIKE

Nat was fifteen, and his life was not going well. He had always hated school and found writing difficult, and things were just mounting up. The school he went to was a caring school, and his parents, the counsellor and the principal knew each other and could talk comfortably. They met and decided that if Nat could find a job, they would arrange an exemption. Perhaps he was one of those boys who would be happier in the adult world than the in-between world of high school.

Luckily Nat scored a job, in a one-man pizza shop – 'Stan's Pizza' – and left school. Stan, who was about thirty-five, was doing a good trade and needed help. Nat went to work there and loved it. His voice deepened, he stood taller, his bank balance grew. His parents, though, began to worry for a new reason. Nat planned to buy a motorbike – a big bike – to get to work. Their home was up a winding, slippery road in the mountains. They watched in horror as his savings got closer to the price of the motorcycle. They suggested a car, to no avail. Time passed.

One day Nat came home and, in the way of teenage boys, muttered something sideways as he walked past the dinner table. Something about a car. They asked him to repeat it, not sure if they should. 'Oh, I'm not going to get a bike. I was talking to Stan. Stan reckons a bloke'd be an idiot to buy a motorbike living up here. He reckons I should wait an' get a car.'

'Thank God for Stan!' thought his parents, but outwardly they just smiled and went on eating their meal.

mentoring – sports coaches, uncles, teachers and bosses – rarely understand their role and often do it badly. Mentoring used to take place in the workplace, especially under the apprenticeship system, where a young man learned a great deal about attitudes and responsibilities along with his trade skills. This has all but disappeared. You won't get much mentoring while working weekends at the local supermarket!

Enlisting the help of others

The years from fourteen until the early twenties are for moving into the adult world, for separating from parents. Parents carefully and watchfully ease back. This is the time when a son develops a life which is quite separate from the family. He has teachers you barely know, experiences you never hear about and faces challenges that you cannot help him with. Pretty scary stuff.

A fourteen- or sixteen-year-old is far from ready to just be 'out there'. There have to be others to act as a bridge, and this is what mentors do. We should not leave youngsters in a peer group at this age without adult care. But a mentor is more than a teacher or a coach: a mentor is special to the child and the child is special to him. A sixteen-year-old will not always listen to his parents – his inclination is not to. But a mentor is different. This is a time for the youngster to make his 'glorious mistakes', and part of the mentor's job is to make sure the mistakes are not fatal.

Parents have to ensure that mentoring happens – and they should have a big hand in choosing who does it. It really helps to belong to a strong social group – an active church, a family-minded sport, a community-oriented school or a group of friends who really care about each other.

You need to have these kinds of friends to provide what uncles and aunts used to – someone who cares about and enjoys your kids. These friends can show an interest in your youngsters, ask them about their views. Hopefully they will make your kids welcome in their homes, 'kick their bums' occasionally and be a listening ear when things at home are a little tense. (Many a mother has experienced a big fight with her teenage daughter who then runs off to tell her woes to her mum's best friend down the road. This is what friends are for!)

You can do the same for their kids, too. Teenagers are quite enjoyable when they are not your own!

Isolated kids are in danger

Teenagers suffer badly if their parents are isolated. I know this from experience. When my parents migrated to Australia, they were already shy people and became even shyer once we were there. They never found a peer group or friendship circle into which we kids could expand gradually. As a result, when my sister and I hit our mid-teens, we had to break out into the big world in dramatic and risky ways. Some young people come to real grief in this way – becoming mentally ill, suicidal or anorexic. Others rebel so strongly that they end up in a peer group which exposes them to drugs, crime or sexual predation. If you're a parent of teenagers, you must push yourself to get out and be part of the community, creating a social network for your kids. You cannot be a hermit and raise kids well.

What if there is no mentor available?

If there are no mentors around, then a young man will fall into a lot of potholes on the road to adulthood. He may fight needlessly with his parents in trying to establish himself as independent. He may just become withdrawn and depressed. Kids at this age have so many dilemmas and decisions – about sexuality, career choices or what to do about drugs and alcohol. If Mum and Dad keep spending time with them, and are in touch with their world, then kids will keep talking to them about these things. But sometimes there will be a need to talk to other adults, too. In one study, it was shown that just one good adult friend outside the family was a significant preventative of juvenile crime. (As long as the friend isn't *into* crime!)

Young men will try their best to find structure and direction in their lives. They may choose born-again religion or an Eastern cult, disappear onto the Internet, follow music, sport, or gang membership. If we don't have a community for kids to belong to, they will make their own. But a community made up only of the peer group is not enough – it may be just a group of lost souls, without the skills or knowledge to help its members. Many boys' friendship circles are really just loose collections which offer very little sharing or emotional support.

The worst thing we can do with adolescents is to leave them alone. This is why we need those really great school teachers, sport coaches, scout leaders, youth workers and many other sources of adult involvement at this age. We need enough so that there is someone special for every kid – a tall order.

Today we mostly get mothering right, and fathering is undergoing a great resurgence. Finding good mentors for the kids in our community is the next big hurdle.

In a nutshell

1 In the years between birth and six, boys need lots of affection so they can 'learn to love'. Talking and teaching one-to-one helps them connect to the world. The mother is usually the best person to provide this, although a father can take this part.

2 At about the age of six, boys show a strong interest in maleness, and the father becomes the primary parent. His interest and time become critical. The mother's part remains important, however, and she shouldn't 'back off' from her son just because he is older.

3 From about fourteen years of age, boys need mentors – other adults who care about them personally and help them move gradually into the larger world. Old societies provided initiation to mark this stage, and mentors were much more available.

4 Single mothers can raise boys well but must search carefully for good, safe, male role-models and must devote some time to self-care (since they are doing the work of two).

Special announcement: gender differences are real!

The fashionable theory for the last thirty years has been that boys and girls have no differences other than those that we give them through condition- ing. According to this thinking, all differences in gender arise from the clothes and toys we give  them, and so on. Well-meaning parents and lots of pre-schools and schools got quite fanatical about this: working hard to get the boys to play with dolls and the girls into the Lego. It was felt that if we raised all children the same then gender differences and prob- lems would disappear.

The aim was to break out of old stereotypes – that a girl could only be a nurse or secretary, while a boy could be a doctor, businessman or soldier. This was an important social change – perhaps the most important of the twentieth century.

Any idea that there might be in-built biological differences between girls and boys was anathema to this idea, and thinking

about it was discouraged. Some terrible things had been done in the name of biology. For instance, well into this century it was argued that, as women had smaller brains, they were not fit for tasks other than housework or motherhood! (After all, motherhood requires few brains!) This was extended to women not being allowed to vote, get equal pay, own property and so on. To achieve equality for women in the 1970s and 1980s, it was important to argue that women were born equal to men. Research into gender differences became a taboo subject, because nobody wanted to be seen to be setting back the cause of women's liberation.

Nowadays some shades of grey are beginning to emerge. There is a willingness to see that some differences do exist which are not socially created, and that these differences are okay – they don't mean girls are better than boys or vice versa. If a girl's brain develops more quickly than a boy's then we can plan accordingly so this difference isn't a problem. If a boy at school prefers to be given clear instructions – while a girl prefers to work cooperatively in a team – then we can accommodate them both. If a boy likes to use his body and a girl likes to use words then we can help them to understand each other and 'speak each other's language'. We can have less blame and more understanding.

In the next two chapters we will look at two major differences that are very significant in learning to help our sons grow up well:

- how hormones (such as testosterone) influence boys' behaviour, and what to do about it:
- how boys' and girls' brains grow differently and affect their ways of behaving and thinking.

KNOWING THE DIFFERENCES

Some of the real gender differences are so obvious that it's amazing they were overlooked. For example, the average boy has 30 percent more muscle bulk than the average girl. Boys are stronger and their bodies are more inclined to action. They even have more red blood cells (the original red-blooded boy!). It has nothing to do with gender conditioning. We have to give boys plenty of chance to exercise – girls too if they want it. Boys will need extra help to control themselves from hitting each other and girls. Girls need help to learn not to use their better verbal skills to needle and demean boys. And so on.

This doesn't mean saying 'every boy *must*...' or 'every girl *must*...'. After all, some girls are stronger and more physical than most boys. (Some girls need training in nonviolence. In one school in Australia, parents removed their sons because girls kept hitting them.) Gender differences are generalisations which are true enough of the time to be very helpful.

BOYS AND HEARING

One significant gender difference is that young boys tend to have growing spurts which affect their ear canals. The ear canal stretches, thins and often blocks up, leading to periods of hearing loss. A boy often 'cops it' at school or home for not listening, not doing what he is told. The problem may affect one boy in a class this month and another boy a month later. It's temporary, and it just means you have to make sure boys hear what you are saying to them. Sometimes they're not naughty, just deaf!

Testosterone!

Janine is pregnant – seven weeks pregnant – and very excited. She doesn't know it yet, but her baby is going to be a boy. We say 'going to be', because a foetus doesn't start that way! It may surprise you to know that all young creatures start life being female. The Y chromosome that makes a baby into a boy is an 'add-on' chromosome which starts to act in the womb – to give a boy the extra bits he needs to be a boy and to stop other bits growing. A male is a female with optional extras. That's why everyone has nipples, though not everyone needs them.

The testosterone cycle

In Janine's baby's tiny body, at around the eighth week of pregnancy, the Y chromosomes stir in the cells and testosterone starts being made. As a result of this new chemical presence, the baby starts to become more of a boy – growing testicles and a penis, and making other more subtle changes in his brain and body. Once the testicles are formed (by the fifteenth week they are fully developed) they start to make extra testosterone, too, so he becomes progressively more and more masculine.

WHAT'S THIS ?

If Janine is *very* stressed her body may suppress the testosterone in baby Jamie's body, and he may not develop fully his penis and testicles, and so will be incompletely developed at birth. He will catch up, however, in the first year.

After birth, young Jamie will have as much testosterone in his bloodstream as a twelve-year-old boy! He needed all this testosterone to stimulate his body to develop male qualities in time to be born. This 'testosterone hangover' will result in him having little erections from time to time as a newborn.

A few months after birth, the testosterone level will drop off to about a fifth of the birth levels, and throughout toddlerhood the levels stay pretty low. Boy and girl toddlers (I'm sure you'd agree) behave pretty much the same.

At the age of *four*, for reasons nobody quite understands, boys receive a sudden surge of testosterone – doubling their blood levels. At this age, little Jamie may become much more interested in action, heroics, adventures and vigorous play. His dad may well find that this age is a good one because Jamie can now play ball games, they can do gardening together, and interact in ways that were not possible when he was little and helpless.

At *five* years of age, the testosterone level drops by a half, and young Jamie calms down again, just in time for school! Enough testosterone is still around for him to be interested in activity, adventure and exploration, but not especially in girls.

Somewhere between the ages of *eleven* and *thirteen*, the levels start to rise sharply again. Eventually they will increase by some 800 percent over the levels of toddlerhood. The result is a sudden growth and elongation of his arms and legs – so much that his whole nervous system has to rewire itself. (For computer buffs, it's a little like installing the latest version of Windows!) In about 50 percent of boys, the testosterone levels are so high that some converts into oestrogen, and breast swelling and tenderness may be experienced. This is nothing to worry about.

Brains go out the window

The reorganisation of Jamie's brain, caused by the rapid growth, makes him dopey and disorganised for many months. His mother and father have to act as his substitute brain for a while! If they're not aware of the reasons for this, parents can wonder where they have gone wrong. If Jamie's parents know this is all part of puberty and take a relaxed, if vigilant, attitude then things should work out just fine.

By age *fourteen*, the testosterone level is now at a peak, and pubic hair, acne, strong sexual feelings and general restlessness may well drive Jamie and everyone around him slightly crazy.

When Jamie reaches his *midtwenties*, things settle down, hormonally speaking. His testosterone levels are just as high, but his body has become used to them and he is not quite so reactive.

are a little more under control! The hormone continues him with male features well into later life – such as high cholesterol, baldness, hairy nostrils and so on! On the plus side, the testosterone gives him surges of creative energy, a love of competition, and a desire to achieve and to be protective. Hopefully his energies will be channelled into activities and career choices (as well as a happy sex life) which bring all kinds of satisfaction and benefits.

In his early *forties*, Jamie's levels of testosterone begin a very gradual decline. He goes for days at a time without thinking about sex! In the bedroom, quality replaces quantity. Jamie now has less to prove, and is more mellow and wise. He assumes quiet leadership in group and work situations. He values friendship and makes his best contributions to the world.

Each boy is different

What we have described here is the pattern for the average boy. There is wide variation among males and also lots of overlap between the sexes. Some girls will have more testosterone-type behaviour than some boys, and some boys will show more oestrogen-type behaviour than some girls. Nonetheless, the general pattern will hold true for most children.

Understanding boys' hormones and their effects means we can understand what is going on and be sympathetic and helpful. Just as a good husband understands his partner's PMT (premenstrual tension), a good parent of a boy understands his TNT (testosterone needing tuition).

Why boys scuffle and fight

Testosterone also affects mood and energy – it is more than just a growth hormone. There's no doubt it causes energetic and boisterous behaviour. That's why, for centuries, horses were gelded to make them better behaved. Testosterone, injected into female rats, makes them try to mate with other female rats and fight with each other. It makes certain parts of the brain grow and others slow down in growth. It can grow more muscles and less fat, and it can make you go bald and bad tempered!

How testosterone affects the psychology of males can be illustrated by a famous study. A tribe of monkeys in a laboratory was closely observed to learn about its social structure. Researchers found that the male monkeys had a definite hierarchy or pecking order. The females' hierarchy was looser and more relaxed, and based on who groomed whose hair! But the males always knew who was boss, and sub-boss, and sub-sub-boss, and had frequent fights to prove it.

Once the researchers had worked out the monkey dynamics, they set about to stir up trouble. They captured the lowest-ranking male monkey and gave him an injection of testosterone. Then they put him back with the tribe. You can guess what happened next. He started a boxing match with his 'immediate superior'. Much to his own surprise, he won! So he went and took on the

next monkey! Within twenty minutes he had worked his way up and tossed off the biggest monkey from the highest branch. Our hero was small, but he had **testosterone!** He became the 'acting manager'.

Sadly for him, this was not to last. The injection soon

wore off, and our little hero was knocked back all the way down to the bottom of the heap. One wag at a seminar called out during this story, 'Sounds like the Conservative Party!' I can't really comment on this!

The point is that testosterone influences the brain and makes boys more concerned with rank and competition.

Boys need order

In their book *Raising a Son*, Don and Jeanne Elium tell the story of an old scoutmaster who comes and sorts out a hopelessly rowdy scout troop in their city. This is the scout troup from hell: the boys are always fighting and damaging the hall, nothing is being learned and many gentler boys have left the troop. It's time for a clean sweep. On his first night with the troop, the scoutmaster sets some rules, invites a couple of boys to shape up or leave, brings in a clear structure and begins teaching skills in an organised way. He successfully turns the group around. In a couple of months it is thriving.

The scoutmaster explained to the Eliums that in his experience there are three things boys always need to know:

1 Who's in charge?
2 What are the rules?
3 Will those rules be fairly enforced?

The key word is structure

Boys feel insecure and in danger if there isn't enough structure in a situation. If no-one is in charge, they begin jostling with each other to establish the pecking order. Their testosterone-driven make-up leads them to want to set up hierarchies, but they can't always do it because they are all the same age. If we provide structure, then they can relax. For girls, this is not so much of a problem.

Several years ago I spent time in the slums of Calcutta to learn about families there. At first glance, Calcutta seemed chaotic and frightening. In fact, though, there were gang-lords and neighbourhood hier-archies – and these, for better or worse, provided a structure for people to live their lives. You were safer with a structure – even a mafia-like structure – than with none. As a better structure was provided, by reli-gious or community leaders who were trustworthy and competent, then life got even

better. Wherever you see a gang of boys looking unruly, you know the adult leadership is failing. Boys form gangs for survival. It's their attempt to have a sense of belonging, order and safety.

Boys act tough to cover up their fear. If someone is clearly the boss, they relax. But the boss must not be erratic or punitive. If the person in charge is a bully, the boys' stress levels rise, and it's back to the law of the jungle. If the teacher, scoutmaster or parent is kind and fair (as well as being strict) then boys will drop their 'macho' act and get on with learning.

This seems to be an in-built gender difference. If girls are anx-ious in a group setting they tend to cower and be quiet, whereas boys respond by running about, making a lot of noise. This has been mistakenly seen as boys 'dominating the space' in nursery schools and so on. However, it is actually an anxiety response. Schools which are very good at engaging boys in interesting and concrete activities (such as Montessori schools, where there is a lot of structural work with blocks, shapes, beads and so on) do not experience this gender difference in children's behaviour.

Not everyone accepts that hormones affect boys' behaviour. Some feminist biologists have argued that men have testosterone through conditioning – that it comes from being raised that way. There is actually a partial truth in this. One study found that boys in scary or violent school environments produced more testosterone. When the same school introduced a more supportive environment (where teachers did not abuse or threaten, where bullying was tackled with special programmes) then the boys' levels of testosterone dropped measurably. So environment *and* biology both played a part.

But environment only influences the hormone. Nature – and boys' inbuilt calendar – creates it. Success with boys means accepting their nature while directing it in good ways. Trying to turn boys into girls is doomed to failure.

How did male and female differences come about?

Evolution is constantly changing the shape of all living creatures. For instance, early humans had huge jaws and teeth for chewing raw food. But when fires and cooking were discovered, over many generations our jaws and teeth became smaller because our food was softer to chew. So our behaviour has actually changed our physical shape. If we have a few thousand years of eating fast food we may end up chinless altogether!

Some gender differences are obvious in human beings – size, hairiness and so on. But the main differences are the hidden ones. These came about through taking very different roles for a very large part of our history. Hunter–gatherer societies divided the work very much along gender lines. For 99 percent of human history, the women mostly gathered, and the men mostly hunted.

Hunting was a specialised activity. It required quick team action, sudden and strong muscular activity in short bursts, and

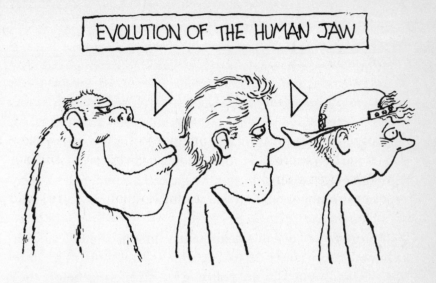

EVOLUTION OF THE HUMAN JAW

you had to be very single-minded. Once the chase was on, there was no time for discussion. Someone was in charge, and you did what you were told or else.

The women's work of gathering seeds, roots and insects was different. It gave time for discussion, required finger dexterity and sensitivity, and included the care of babies and children. As a result, all human females have finger sensitivity several times greater than males. The women's work required caution, constancy and attention to detail – whereas hunting required a certain degree of recklessness or even self-sacrifice. Women's bodies became generally smaller but better able to persist and endure. Men's bodies were better at rapid bursts of strength but more likely to be laid low by a dose of 'flu or an ingrown toenail! The differences were not great, and some role flexibility probably helped. So we ended up a species with slight but significant differences between male and female bodies and brains.

The hunter–gatherer tradition continues to have a problematic legacy. In the third world (where people now live by agriculture), the men often do not work as hard as the women. Presumably they are waiting to fight someone or hunt something!

The links between sex and aggression

There is some support from primate studies for the idea that males with more power have higher sex drives. Men in sports teams that win have a higher testosterone level (after the game) than those who lose. And, according to historians, many great leaders (President Kennedy, for instance) had very high sex drives, to a degree that was really rather tragic and disabling. (It's kind of hard to run a country when you want to keep racing off to have sex all the time.)

One study of juvenile delinquency in the 1980s found an intriguing connection – that boys were several times more likely to get into trouble with the police in the six months before their first sexual experience. In other words, they calmed down a bit once they started having sex. Since all boys masturbate at this age, it can't just have been the release of sexual frustration. But perhaps the boys felt they had 'joined the human race' when they found a real-life lover. (We don't recommend this as a cure for crime, but it makes sense.)

Sex and aggression are somewhat linked – controlled by the same centres in the brain and by the same hormone group. This has been the source of enormous human tragedy and suffering, inflicted in sexual assaults on women, children and men. Because of this connection, it is very important that boys

are helped to relate to women as people, to have empathy and to learn to be good lovers.

It's never an excuse for male aggression to blame hormones. But it's vital that we separate the stimuli of violence from the stimuli of sex. We shouldn't really make or show movies which link the two. The rape–revenge plot of many B-grade movies is a bad connection to make.

Even adult men can get the wrong idea. A matchmaking agency recently had to counsel a man in his sixties who was being far too sexually forward on 'dates' that the agency arranged. The man, a very gentle and considerate person (widowed two years earlier), had researched copies of *Cosmopolitan* magazine to find out what today's women liked, and was acting accordingly!

Porn movies are just as bad. The typical porn movie is just plain silly – rather unappealing people just grinding away. Where are the movie depictions of tender, sensuous, playful and boisterous lovemaking (with plots that include conversation, sharing and vulnerability), so that mid-adolescent boys can learn a fuller kind of sexuality?

Overcoming sexual violence probably starts younger still. It may just come down to treating children more kindly. Raymond Wyre, an expert on working with men who sexually abuse children, found in his work that while not every sex offender had been the victim of sexual assault (though many had), everyone without exception had been the recipient of a very cruel and uncaring childhood. It was the lack of empathy, resulting from never having been shown consistent understanding and kindness, which he felt was the key factor in someone being able to sexually assault another human being.

Guiding the 'high drive' boys

Testosterone provides energy and focus. A boy with high levels of the hormone makes good leadership material. Early in the school year, teachers often notice a certain kind of boy who will either become a hero of the class or a complete villain. For this boy there is no middle ground. This type of boy stands out by his:

- challenging behaviour and competitiveness;
- greater physical maturity;
- high energy levels.

If the teacher is able to befriend such a boy and direct his energies in good ways, then the boy will thrive and be a plus in the school. If a teacher or parent ignores, backs off or is negative towards the boy, then the boy's pride will depend on defeating the adult and problems will compound. These boys have leadership potential, but leadership has to be taught from an early age.

In a nutshell

1 Testosterone in varying degrees affects every boy. It gives him growth spurts, makes him want to be active, and makes him competitive and in need of strong guidelines and a safe, ordered environment.

2 It triggers significant changes:
- at four – into activity and boyishness;
- at thirteen – into rapid growth and disorientation; and
- at fourteen – into testing limits and breaking through to early manhood.

3 The boy with testosterone in his bloodstream likes to know who is the boss but also must be treated fairly. Bad environments bring out the worst in him. The boy with lots of testosterone needs special help to develop leadership qualities and channel his energies in good ways.

4 A boy needs to learn empathy and feeling and be shown tenderness if he is to be a sexually caring being.

5 Some girls have a lot of testosterone but, on the whole, it's a boy thing – and needs our understanding, not blame or ridicule. Testosterone equals vitality, and it's our job to honour it and steer it into healthy directions.

TESTOSTERONE MAKES YOU COMPLETE!

Amazing testosterone facts

- In the animal kingdom, one kind of hyena – the spotted hyena – is born with so much testosterone that even the female pups have a pseudo penis and their labia resemble testicles. The spotted hyenas are born with a full set of teeth,  and the pups are so aggressive that they often eat each other within a day or two of being born!

- In a rare condition of boy babies, which is found in the Dominican Republic, testosterone does not take effect in the womb because of a missing enzyme. These boys are born without a penis or testicles, looking in fact more like girls, and they are raised as such. But at about twelve years of age, testosterone is produced in their body and the boys suddenly develop into 'real' boys, growing a penis and testicles, getting a deep voice and so on. They apparently then live normal lives as men. They are known in their language as 'penis at twelve' children.

- A condition called Congenital Adrenal Hyperplasia can give girls excess testosterone in the womb, but this is remedied once the child is born. Though they are hormonally normal from then on, these girls show above-average athletic skills, as well as a preference for male playmates, toy cars and guns, and 'masculine' clothes.

- An excess sensitivity to testosterone, or an excess of it, has been linked significantly to mathematical ability, left-handedness and a very high incidence of asthma and allergies.

- Oestrogen – the female counterbalancing hormone to testosterone – has been shown to cause nerve cells to grow more connections. Females have smaller brains, but these are better connected!

- Baritone singers in Welsh choirs have more testosterone than tenor singers. Baritones are also more sexually active!

- Making love raises your testosterone level. The more you get the more you want – at least for a couple of days! Winning at sport or politics raises your testosterone level. Stress and loneliness lower it. They lead to more oestrogen being produced so you can cope like a woman!

- One final testosterone fact – perhaps the most amazing of all – illustrates the intricate dance between biology and behaviour in the development of higher animals. Are you ready? Here goes...

    Mother rats frequently lick the genitals of their male babies, and this helps their brains to become fully male.

    And guess what? It's the presence of testosterone in the urine of the baby male rats that seems to trigger the behaviour. If baby female rats are given testosterone injections, the mother licks their genitals too! If baby boy rats are castrated, the mothers don't lick them any more. (A double tragedy!)

But wait, it gets more amazing. The rats that are licked in this way develop a masculine-functioning pituitary gland, whether they are male or female. Female rats given the licking treatment behaved like male rats for the rest of their lives. When the licking was replaced by an experimenter stroking the male or female rats with a paintbrush each day, the same long-term physical changes to the brain took place as a result.

Of the hundreds of studies I have seen, this one probably tells us more about how complex the interaction is between nature and nurture in developing gender characteristics. (And that is perhaps the only conclusion we can draw from it!)

There are physical and social influences at work all the time, in complex interaction, to produce healthy and functioning males and females. Gender differentiation does not just happen automatically. Without affection and stimulation, we know children don't grow as well or become as intelligent as their potentials would allow. We have to bring nurturing and parenting skills to bear, both to help our kids develop physically and find a comfortable gender identity.

CHAPTER 4

How boys' and girls' brains differ

A miracle of growth

The brain of a baby in the womb grows very rapidly, developing in a month or two from just a few cells into one of the most complex structures in nature. By the sixth month of pregnancy a foetus has impressive abilities, all controlled by its brain – such as recognising your voice, responding to movements, even kicking back when prodded! It can be seen with ultrasound to be actually moving its mouth as if it is singing in the womb.

SINGING IN THE WOMB
JUST SINGING IN THE WOMB !

At birth the brain is still only partially formed – and only a third of its eventual size. It takes a long time for the brain to be completed. For instance, the language part of the brain is not fully formed until about the age of thirteen. (This is why it is so important that boys are kept up with reading through the primary school years.)

From very early on, gender differences are evident in the unborn baby's brain. One difference is that a baby boy's brain develops more slowly than a baby girl's. Another difference is that the left and right sides form fewer connections in a boy.

All animal brains have two halves. In simple animals (like lizards or birds) this means that everything is duplicated. A bang on the head might wipe out part of one half of the brain, but the other half can take care of things! However, in humans (who have a lot more to think about!), the two brain halves specialise somewhat. One half handles language and reasoning, and the other movement, emotion and the senses of space and position. Both halves talk to each other through a big central bundle of fibres called the corpus callosum (which sounds like the name of a Catholic school). The corpus callosum in boys is proportionately smaller in size – there are fewer connections running from one side to the other.

It has been shown in recent studies that boys tend to attack certain kinds of problems (such as a spelling quiz or word puzzle) using only one side of their brain, while girls use **both** sides. This can be vividly seen using the brain-scanning technology of magnetic resonance (MRI). The 'lights go on' all over a girl's brain, while in a boy they tend to be localised on one part of one side only. This has enormous ramifications (examined later on).

Why the difference?

The brain of a baby before and after birth grows rather like a tub of alfalfa sprouts accidentally left in the sun – brain cells keep getting longer and making new connections all the time. The left half of the cortex grows more slowly than the right in all human babies, but in males it is even slower still. The testosterone in a boy's bloodstream slows things down. Oestrogen, the hormone that is predominant in the bloodstream of baby girls, actually stimulates faster growth of brain cells.

As the right half grows, it tries to make connections with the left half of the brain. In boys, the left half isn't ready yet to take the connections, and so the nerve cells reaching across from the right cannot find a place to 'plug in'. So they go back to the right side where they came from and plug in there instead. As a result, the right half in a boy's brain is richer in internal connections but poorer in cross connections to the other half. This is one possible explanation of boys' greater success in mathematics, which is largely a 'right side of the brain' activity (and their greater interest

in taking machinery to pieces and leaving the bits lying around!). But we must be careful not to overdo these conclusions, as sometimes parental expectations, practice, and social pressure also influence skills and abilities. It's clear that practice actually helps more brain connections to be laid down permanently, so encouragement and teaching actually affect the shape and power of the brain in later life.

Whether the cause is hormonal or environmental, there is no doubt that these brain differences exist between men and women today. Because of their more connected brain halves, women who suffer strokes usually recover more speedily and completely than men. They can activate extra pathways to the other half of their brain to do the job of the damaged parts. Girls who have learning problems improve quicker with tuition for the same reason. And boys are more prone to problems resulting from brain damage at birth, and so on. This may explain the greater numbers of boys with learning difficulties, autism and many other disorders.

There are other brain differences which are poorly understood. Seven distinct areas of difference have been found through autopsy or through computer imaging.

LEARNING TO COMMUNICATE

PRACTICAL HELP

Communication is essential to life. Yet sadly, in every classroom, there are about four or five children who can't read, write or speak well. And among these children boys outnumber girls by four to one! This is now thought to be the result of boys' brains not being quite so well organised for language.

But there is no need to just let this be. If you want to prevent your child having learning or language problems there is a lot you can do to help, according to neuroscientist Dr Jenny Harasty and team, who have done ground-breaking research into understanding communication disorders.

Dr Harasty found that in females, two regions of the brain dedicated to handling language are proportionately 20 percent to 30 percent larger than in males. But no-one knows whether these regions are larger at birth, or because girls get more practice at using them. Whatever the cause, we do know that the brain is very responsive to learning experiences if these are given at the right age. And for language, that age is zero to eight. In adolescence and adulthood we go on learning, but the

older the child, the harder it is to change that early wiring of the brain.

You can help your boy learn to communicate better, starting right from when he is a baby. This means that he will be a better reader, writer and speaker when he goes to school. Here's how ...

1 'TALK THEM UP' – ONE STEP AT A TIME

Children acquire spoken language one step at a time. Babies under one year of age will begin to babble and gesture very enthusiastically, telling us they are ready to learn verbal communication! This is the time to start to teach them words.

- With a baby who babbles, repeat a word that seems to be what they mean. Baby says 'gukuk, baguk!' and points to his toy duck. You say 'Ducky! John's ducky!' Soon John will be saying 'Ducky' too.

- With a toddler who says single words, like 'milk!' you say a couple ➤

of words, such as, 'milk bottle'. This helps him to move on to joining pairs of words together, and so on.

- A child who is saying words in twos and threes can be stretched further by imitating you in whole sentences. For example, he says 'Gavin truck!' You reply, 'Gavin wants a truck? Here's Gavin's truck!' And so on.

In short, kids learn best if you speak back to them *one step ahead* of the stage they are at. And they love the game. All human beings love to communicate.

GOOD-
NOW
AMPLIFIER

REMOTE CONTROL

2 EXPLAIN THINGS TO CHILDREN EVERY CHANCE YOU CAN

This is a great use of the many times when you are just doing routine things with your children – travelling, doing housework, going for a walk. Chatter, explain, answer questions. Surprisingly, some very loving parents (who care for their kids well) seem not to realise that kids' brains grow from conversation. Don't be shy – explain things, tell them stories, chatter to them! For example, 'You see this lever? This makes the wipers go. They swish the rain away from the window'. 'This vacuum cleaner makes a big wind. It sucks the air and pulls the dirt into a bag. Would you like a turn?'

This kind of talk – provided you don't overdo it and bore your child senseless – does more for your child's brain than any amount of expensive education later on.

3 READ TO YOUR KIDS FROM AN EARLY AGE

Even when your child is just one year old, you can enjoy books together – especially the kind that have rhymes and repetition. 'Humpty Dumpty' and 'Twinkle Twinkle Little Star' work just fine. From enjoying them at your knee, children learn to love books, look at the pictures and enjoy the sound of your voice. You can 'ham it up' a little by making funny voices or being dramatic. Have the child on your knee or lie in bed together at bedtime.

As your child gets to have favourite stories, you can play a 'predicting' game ... 'And the little cat went ... ?' pausing so your child provides the 'Miaow!' Prediction is a very important part of reading. Good readers anticipate what word is coming next.

Remember, whenever playing learning games with kids, the trick is to be playful, making your children 'stretch' their minds just a little – which they will love to do.

All kids benefit from these three learning games – but for boys it is a preventive step because of their disposition to be poorer at language if we don't help them along. And it's fun to do, anyway!

Dr Jenny Harasty advises that if you have worries about your boy's speech and language development (if he isn't talking as well as you think he should) trust your intuition. Speak to a speech pathologist from your local hospital or community health centre. Sessions of speech therapy are fun for children and can make all the difference to a good start.

Why is it important to know about brains?

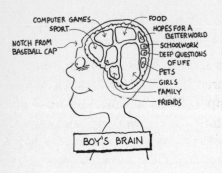

COMPUTER GAMES
SPORT
NOTCH FROM
BASEBALL CAP
FOOD
HOPES FOR A
BETTER WORLD
SCHOOLWORK
DEEP QUESTIONS
OF LIFE
PETS
GIRLS
FAMILY
FRIENDS

BOY'S BRAIN

Knowing about the differences in boys' brains helps to explain some practical difficulties that boys have, and what to do about them.

If your brain is somewhat less connected from right to left, then you will have trouble doing things well which need both sides of the brain. This involves skills such as *reading*, *talking about feelings* and solving problems through *quiet introspection* rather than by beating people over the head! Do these problems sound at all familiar to you? So now can you see the importance of all this brain research?

Danger: sexism alert!

There is a vitally important point to be made here. To say that 'boys are different' can very easily turn into an excuse for saying 'they are defective' or, worse still, 'they can't help it'. The same sort of generalisations were once applied to girls: 'They'll never be any good at science or engineering', 'They're too emotional to be in responsible jobs', and so on. So please take the following points on board very seriously:

- the differences are slight for most people;
- they are only tendencies;
- they don't apply to every individual; and
- most important of all, we don't have to accept them as limitations.

Helping the brain to grow

We can work to help boys read better, express themselves better, solve conflicts better and empathise better – and so help them to be great human beings. Schools have equity programmes to help girls in mathematics and sciences so they have access to these careers. We are now beginning to see that we can help boys with English, Drama and so on, which can better equip them to live in the modern world. (For some great ways to do this, see the chapter on schools, 'A revolution in schooling'.)

Our brains are brilliant and flexible devices, always able to learn. A parent can teach a boy how to avoid getting into fights by working out better ways to join in a game or solve a dispute peacefully. They can help a boy learn skills like:

- how to figure out people's feelings from the expressions on their faces;
- how to make friends and join in a game or conversation;
- how to read his own body signals – for example, to know when he is getting angry and needs to walk away from a situation.

By working on these skills with their sons, parents are building connections from one side of their son's brain to the other.

In school the same help is needed. One maths teacher I know rarely lets a lesson pass without using some practical, hands-on example of what was being studied – often going outside to do it in a practical way. He found that the unmotivated ones among his students could get a grasp of the con-

cepts if they could see them in practice and do physical things with their bodies to comprehend the idea being taught. They were getting right-brain concepts to link to their left-brain understanding – using their strengths to overcome their weaknesses.

Starting school: why boys should start later

At the age of six or seven, when children start serious schooling, boys are six to twelve months less developed mentally than girls. They are especially delayed in what is called 'fine-motor coordination', which is the ability to use their fingers carefully and hold a pen or scissors. And since they are still in the stage of 'gross-motor' development, they will be itching to move their large muscles around – so they will not be good at sitting still.

In talking to heads of infant departments (from country schools in outback Australia to big international schools in Europe and Asia) the same message comes through: 'Boys should stay back a year'. It's great for children – boys and girls – to go to nursery school from four or five years of age, since they need the social stimulation and wider experiences it provides (and because parents need a break!). But the boys should stay there longer – up to a year longer in some cases. For most, this would mean that they move through school being *a year older than the girl in the next desk.* Which also means that they are, intellectually speaking, on a par with her. Eventually boys catch up with girls intellectually but, in the way schools work now, the damage is already done. The boys feel themselves to be failures, they miss out on key skills because they are just not ready and so get turned off from learning.

In early primary school, boys (whose motor nerves are still growing) actually get signals from their body saying, 'Move around. Use me'. To a stressed-out teacher, this looks like misbehaviour. A boy sees that his craft work, drawing and writing are not as good as the girls', and thinks, 'This is not for me!'. He quickly switches off from learning – especially if there is not a male teacher available. 'School is for girls', he tells himself.

If we take note of recent brain research, there are other ways we can design schools to be much better places for boys. This is explored in the chapter on schools, 'A revolution in schooling'.

Boys are not inferior – just different

Having a well-developed right side of the brain, as boys tend to do, has many pluses. As well as having mathematical and mechanical abilities, males tend to be action-oriented – if they see a problem, they want to fix it. The right side of the brain handles both feelings and actions, so men are more likely to take action while women tend to mull over something to the point of total paralysis! It requires extra effort for a man to shift into his left hemisphere and find the words to explain the feelings he is registering in his right hemisphere.

Germaine Greer has pointed out that there are more male geniuses in many fields, even though many may be imbalanced characters on the whole, needing someone to look after them (usually a woman)!

In an anti-male era, it's important to remember (and to show boys) that men built the planes, fought the wars, laid the railroad tracks, invented the cars, built the hospitals, invented the medicines and sailed the ships that made it all happen. There's an African saying, 'Women hold up half the sky'. But, clearly, men hold up the other half.

A new kind of man

The world no longer needs men who can wrestle with buffaloes. In the modern world, where manual or mechanical labour is less and less important, we need to take that masculine ability and energy and redirect it to a different kind of heroic effort. This means adding language and feeling skills to the thinking and doing skills of boys – making a kind of 'superboy' who is flexible across all kinds of skill areas.

If you think about it, the great men of history – Gandhi, Martin Luther King, Buddha, Jesus – actually were like this. They had courage and determination, along with sensitivity and love for others. It's an unbeatable mix, and it is certainly needed today.

In a nutshell

The gender differences created by male hormones and male genes need to be handled in practical ways. The following sums up what you can do with your boy to help him be a 'new kind of man'.

BECAUSE BOYS OFTEN:	WE NEED TO:
... are prone to separation anxiety ...	... show them as much affection as we do girls, and avoid separations, such as leaving them in childcare before the age of three.
... have testosterone surges making them sometimes argumentative and restless – especially around age fourteen ...	... calmly guide them through conflicts – settle them down with reasoning, not yelling at or attacking them. Be clear that they need to show good manners always, and never use or threaten violence. Fathers need to be role-models and insist that mothers are respected.
... have growth spurts that make them vague and disorganised, especially at age thirteen. (This applies to girls too.) ...	... get involved in organising them, teaching them systems for tidying rooms, doing housework, tackling school projects in small bites, having a routine.
... have bursts of physical energy needing to be expressed ...	... be sure to have lots of space and time for exercise, moving about.
... have a slower rate of brain development, affecting fine motor skills in early primary ...	... delay starting primary school until they have lots of pen-and-paper skills, can handle scissors and so on. ➤

BECAUSE BOYS OFTEN:	WE NEED TO:
... have fewer connections from the language half to the sensory half of the brain...	... read to them, tell them stories, talk to them a lot and explain things, especially from ages one to eight.
... have a need for a clear set of rules, and knowing who is in charge ...	... have good, calm, orderly environments at home and school. Avoid schools where bullying is entrenched.
... have a more muscular body.	... specifically teach them not to hit or hurt others. Also teach them to use words to communicate. (See our book, *More Secrets of Happy Children*, for good discipline methods without hitting, shaming or blaming.)
... have a predisposition to act first without thinking things through.	... talk with them often in a friendly way about options, choices, ways to solve problems and what they can do in situations in their lives.

CHAPTER 5

What dads can do

When my daughter was born by emergency Caesarean, I watched in joy and fear – then grabbed her and hung on to her. That was the deal Shaaron and I had made: no-one else takes this baby!

While Shaaron recovered from the operation over the next few days, I slept on a stretcher on the floor of her hospital room, the baby tucked in beside me – often causing shrieks of shock from change-of-shift nurses who stumbled in at 2 a.m. Sometimes nurses would discreetly take Shaaron aside and ask if this was what she wanted, and she would smile and say, 'Yes, of course!'

Fighting to be a dad

That's kind of how it is for dads these days – you have to fight for the right to **be** a dad. The world doesn't seem to want you to be a parent. They'd rather have you stay late at the office. Someone else will teach your children to hit a ball, play piano and believe in themselves. You just pay the bills, like a good man.

Luckily, fathers are fighting their way back into family life, and very welcome they are too. After all, fathering doesn't have a great tradition in the twentieth century. Our fathers' generation included a few great dads, but most men in those days proved their love by working, not by playing, cuddling, talking or teaching – the things that kids really love. A fair number of dads were violent, scary or drank too much. Many were traumatised by war and were hard to get close to. Some men simply walked out on their families and never came back. So when we come to fathering our own children, it can feel strange – since we may have no knowledge of what good fathering looks like.

All we have are fragments, like a jigsaw with many pieces missing.

Things are looking up. In England, for example, fathers have increased the time they spend with children by 400 percent since the 1960s. As long as you are willing to 'have a go', you will always achieve something. Don't be tempted to leave it all to your partner. The fact is, men bring different things to parenting, things that are unique and irreplaceable. The more you do, the more you will rediscover your talents at fathering and your own unique style. There is nothing as satisfying as raising great kids.

Reviving a lost art

A lot of fathering of boys is simple. Here are some clues:
• Most boys love to be physically active, to have fun with their

fathers. They love to hug their dad, and play wrestle with him. (If they don't like it, you're probably being too rough!)

- They like to accompany you on adventures and experiences in the big, wide world – all the while feeling secure because dad seems so huge and capable (even if he doesn't feel that way himself half of the time).
- They love to hear stories about your life, meet your friends and see what you do for a living.
- They love you to teach them things – anything really. If you don't know things like fishing or making stuff in sheds or fixing go-carts or computers and so on, well, you can learn together. It's trying that counts.

Kids learn your attitudes

Kids don't just learn from what you say to them, they take on your attitudes as well (to a frightening degree). A friend of mine, a Vietnam veteran, was driving with his children and pulled up at

some traffic lights. An Asian family were among those crossing at the lights. My friend's five-year-old suddenly made a racist comment! (I won't quote it here.) But my friend recognised his own words. He was shocked to hear it from a child. It sounded ugly and wrong to him. He found a parking spot and pulled over. He told his child he was sorry that he had ever spoken like that, and he didn't want the child ever to speak like that either.

Kids learn to love by watching you

Children even learn about love by watching you. They love it when you show warmth to their mother, give her a compliment, flirt, exchange a cuddle or a kiss. My daughter cannot resist squeezing in whenever she sees her parents hugging. She loves to soak in the feeling of the two of us. When you are private, and close the bedroom door, children even learn from this some of the awe and mystery of love.

Being respectful to their mother is important. So is being self-respecting – not taking abuse or disrespect but speaking up, making your case. Your son needs to see not only that women are never abused, but that a man can argue calmly, without fighting or lashing out – that he can listen but also make his point and insist on being heard. Sons hate to see their fathers degraded.

Kids learn to feel by watching you

Sons learn about feelings by watching their fathers and other men. They need to see you showing all four of the basic feelings:

sadness	when someone has died or a disappointment has come along;
anger	when something has been unjust or wrong;
happiness	when things go well: and
fear	when there is danger.

There's a balance involved in expressing feelings around our children. Kids need to see that we *have* emotions but (as parents symbolise 'coping') they don't feel safe if we are overwhelmed by them. Use words more than actions. We should speak our anger not act it out. We can share our fears but not get rattled. We can say we are sad and even cry but not become a total sook.

When men have an uncomfortable feeling they often convert it to something more comfortable. Usually anger is the most comfortable feeling for men. When your little boy has got lost in the shopping centre or your teenager has taken a foolish risk, a father who can say, 'I was scared', has much more impact than one who yells and slams doors. If men act angry when they are really sad, scared or even happy this can be pretty confusing for kids.

Boys are trying to match their inner sensations with outer ways of behaving and need us to show them how this is done.

SHOWING OUR FEELINGS

Earlier this year something happened that made me want to cry, and I hesitated, knowing my twelve-year-old son was in the room or close by. I received a phone call telling me that a good friend had terminal cancer. I went into shock, I put the phone down and began to fight back the tears. I walked into the living room, thinking: 'Is this okay? Is this how I want my son to see me?' The answer came back: 'Of course, it's good that he sees me like this.'

I asked my wife for a hug, and stood there holding her and sobbing. I felt my son's approach and then his hand on my shoulder – he was comforting me! The three of us stood there hugging. It was wonderful. Incredible to have things reversed like that.

Perhaps seeing me like that will mean that, when he needs to, he also will have access to the sweet release of tears. I don't want him to be bottled up and volcanic when he meets the inevitable griefs of life. And I don't think he will be. *(A letter from Tony S.)*

STORIES FROM THE HEART

Whatever happens in your marriage, don't divorce your kids

Divorce is a huge blow to a father's hopes and dreams for his children. Some men feel so grief-stricken that they 'cut and run'. Others have to fight the system to stay in contact with their children. It's vitally important – whatever happens to your marriage – that you stay in your children's lives. More and more fathers are sharing parenting equally (or even more so) after divorce. I've talked to men who, after divorce, decided it would be simpler for the children if they didn't main-

tain contact. They always profoundly regretted this decision.

For your children's sake, learn to be polite and kind to your ex-partner, even if you don't always feel it. Better still, work to preserve your partnership by giving that some time and attention too, before it's too late.

~ WHO WAS THAT MASKED MAN ?

Rough-and-tumble games: what's really going on?

There's a unique father behaviour that has been observed all over the world. Dads (along with big brothers, uncles and others) love to wrestle and play rough-and-tumble games with little boys. They can hardly resist it. Australian counsellor Paul Whyte puts it very plainly: 'If you want to get along with boys, learn to wrestle!'

For a long time nobody understood why this was so – especially mothers, who are usually trying to calm things down while dads seem likely to stir them up all over again! But it's been found that what boys are learning in 'rough and tumble' is an essential lesson for all males: how to be able to have fun, get noisy, even get angry and, at the same time, ***know when to stop***. For a male, living with testosterone, this is vital. If you live in a male body, you have to learn how to drive it.

The big male lesson: knowing when to stop

If you've ever wrestled with a little boy, say a three- or four-year-old, it always starts out happily enough. But often, after a minute or two, they 'lose it'. They get angry. Their little jaw starts to jut out! They knit their eyebrows together and (if you haven't spotted the warning signs yet) they start to get serious and hit out with knees and elbows. Ouch!

A dad who knows what he's doing stops the action right there. ***'Hoooooold it! Stop!'*** Then a little lecture takes place – not yelling, just calmly explaining.

'Your body is precious (pointing at boy), and my body is precious too. We can't play this game if somebody might get hurt. So we need a few rules – like, ***No elbowing*** and ***no kneeing or punching!*** Do you understand? Can you handle it?' (Here's a tip: always say 'Can you handle it?' rather than 'Will you keep the rules?', which sounds kind of woosy! No boy is going to say 'No' to a question like 'Can you handle it?'.)

Then you recommence. The young boy is learning a most important life skill – self-control. That he can be strong and excited but can also choose where and when to back off. For males this is very important. In adult life, a man will usually be stronger than his wife or partner. He must know how to not 'lose it', especially when he is angry, tired and frustrated.

For a marriage to survive, it is sometimes necessary for partners to stand nose to nose, both of them yelling at the top of their lungs! This is called 'truth time' – the time when differences that have been building up get aired and cleared up. (We wrote a book about this, called *The Making of Love* [Doubleday, Sydney].)

A woman can't have this kind of honest and intense discussion

WHAT FATHERS DO

(by Jack Kammer)

This could be dangerous, I thought. This is Los Angeles, early June 1992. And, besides, it's getting dark.

Stranded and alone, hauling a heavy suitcase along Washington Boulevard east of Lincoln Avenue, unable to find a phone that made sense or a taxi dispatcher interested in my fare, I was running late for my plane at LAX. I decided that this was a chance I needed, no, *wanted* to take. I approached three young Hispanic men standing outside their car in a fast-food parking lot.

But first a little background. I had just spent four days in the mountains above Palm Springs at a conference of men who wanted to give the nation new hope for old and growing problems. We were a few of the big fish in the small pond that some have called the men's movement. We agreed that what the nation most urgently needs right now is a massive infusion of strong, noble, loving, nurturing, healthy masculine energy to counteract America's malaise, impotence and social pathologies. We talked a lot about the importance of fathers, both as an archetypal metaphor and as a practical reality.

with a man unless she feels absolutely safe with him. She needs to know she will never be hit, and he needs to know in himself that he won't hit. For some couples (it must be said) it's the other way around!

This is the measure of a 'real' man. A real man is one who is in charge of himself and his behaviour. And he begins to learn this, partially at least, while wrestling on the living room floor with Dad or Uncle Pete.

Back in the fast-food parking lot I warily approached the three young, black-haired, brown-skinned men.

'How ya doing?' I said calmly and evenly. 'I'm trying to get to LAX and I'm running late. The cabs and the phones aren't cooperating. How much money would you need to take me?'

They looked at each other. One of them in a white T-shirt said to the one who must have been the driver, 'Go for it, man.' The driver hesitated.

I said, 'Name a price that makes it worth your while.'

He looked straight at me. 'Ten bucks,' he said.

'I'll give you twenty.'

'Let's do it, man,' said the T-shirted youth. The driver nodded and popped the trunk.

'You wanna put your suitcase here?'

'No, thanks,' I answered straight back. The image of being forced empty-handed out of the car was clear in my mind. 'I'd rather keep it with me.'

➤

'That's cool,' the T-shirt said.

So there I was, entrusting my life to what I hoped to be 'positive male energy'. I was thinking we should go west to Lincoln Avenue. We headed east. Now what?

But then we turned south and soon we were on a freeway. I knew it could have been stupid, but I took out my wallet, removed a twenty and said to the driver, 'Here, I want to pay you now'. The driver took it with a simple 'thanks'.

'So here I am, guys,' I said. 'I sure hope you're going to take care of me.'

T-shirt, sitting in the back seat with me, my suitcase between us, smiled knowingly and said, 'It's okay, man. We're good guys.'

I nodded and shrugged. 'I sure hope so, because if you're not, I'm in big trouble, aren't I?'

They all laughed, and then T-shirt spoke up. 'So where you from?'

'Baltimore,' I answered.

'Oh, man, it's nice back east. That's what they say. Green and everything.'

I smiled and nodded, 'Yeah. And back east, LA is our idea of heaven.'

'Naah, it's rough here, man. It's hard.' T-shirt was clearly going to be the spokesman.

Every issue we men's movement guys had talked about during our conference in the mountains was in this car. It was time for a reality check.

'How old are you guys?' I asked.

They were sixteen and seventeen. They were all in school and had part-time jobs. T-shirt and the driver worked in a restaurant. The quiet young man riding shotgun didn't say.

'Tell me about the gangs. Are there gangs at your school?'

'There's gangs everywhere, man. Everywhere. It's crazy.'

'Are you guys in a gang?' I asked.

'No way, man.'

'Why not?' I wondered.

'Because there's no hope in it. You just get a bullet in your head.'

'Yeah, but what hope is there for you outside the gang?'

'I don't know. I just want to get a future. Do something.'

'What's the difference between you guys and the guys in the gangs?'

'I don't know, man. We just don't want to do it.'

'Yeah, but why not? What's the difference?' I gently pressed.

'I don't know, man. I don't know. We're just lucky I guess.'

I let the question sit for a moment, then started up. 'What about fathers? Do you have a father at home?' I asked the youth in the back seat with me.

'Yeah. I do.'

'How about you?' I asked the driver.

'Yeah, I got a dad.'

'Living with you?'

'Yeah.' And the shotgun rider volunteered, 'I got a dad, too.'

'How about the guys in the gangs? Do they have fathers living with them?'

'No way, man. None of them do.'

'So maybe fathers make a difference?' I suggested.

'Absolutely, man. Absolutely.'

'Why?' I probed. 'What difference does a father make?'

'He's always behind you, man, pushing you. Keeping you in line.'

'Yeah. Telling you what's what,' driver and shotgun agreed.

And I was taken safely right where I needed to go. The driver even asked what terminal I wanted. On time. Without a hitch.

I met eighteen amazing men at the conference in the mountains. I am eternally grateful for their wisdom and their urge to heal the nation. But the most amazing men I met on my trip were the three youngest ones, Pablo, Juan and Richard – amazing because, in spite of everything, they were trying to be good.

And the men to whom I am most grateful are the men I never met. The men to whom I am most grateful are their fathers. It was their fathers who got me to the airport. It was their fathers who kept me safe.

Teaching boys to respect women

One day, at around about the age of fourteen, a boy makes a very important discovery. It suddenly occurs to him that he is **bigger than his mother!** Even the sweetest, gentlest boy just can't help thinking it sooner or later: **'She can't make me do it!'**

The thought leads to action and, sooner or later, a boy will try to get the best of Mum by bluffing or intimidating, even in subtle ways. This is an important teaching moment. Don't panic, it isn't necessary to worry or get scared.

Picture this if you will. Fourteen-year-old Sam is in the kitchen. Sam's job is to do the dishes – clear them up, scrape them off, put them in the dishwasher and switch it on. No big deal – he's done it since he was nine. But last night, he didn't finish the job. So, tonight, when his mother goes to get the dishes from the dishwasher (to serve up the meal his father has cooked!) they are in there, unwashed, with green fur growing on them.

Sam's mum naturally pulls him up. 'What's happened?' But tonight Sam is fourteen! He heaves his shoulders back, he stalks about. Perhaps he speaks a little disrespectfully to his mother, under his breath.

Now let's imagine this family is really lucky. One, they have a father. Two, he's home. And, three – he knows his job (we're talking miracles here)!

Sam's father is in the lounge room reading the paper (kind of keeping an overview of things). He picks up on what is going on in the kitchen. This is his cue! Something deep inside him has been waiting for this moment. He folds his paper, strides to the kitchen, and leans on the fridge. Sam can *feel* him come in – it's a kind of primeval moment, hormonal. He can feel the shift of power. The father looks long and hard at Sam and says some time-honoured words – words that *you* probably heard when you were fourteen.

'Don't speak to your mother in that tone of voice … or you'll have me to deal with.'

Now, Sam's mother is a Nineties woman and is quite capable of dealing with Sam. The difference is she is not in it alone. Sam realises that there are two adults here who respect and support each other and who are going to bring him up well.

Most importantly, Sam's mother knows that she does not need to ever feel intimidated in her own home. It's *not* a physical thing between the father and son, but a kind of moral force. If the father is for real, if he respects his partner and he has credibility, then it will work every time, even if some more discussion is needed. The discussion should *not* be about the dishes, but about how to converse respectfully and safely. (If a mother is raising a boy on her own, then things have to take a slightly different tack – and this is discussed in the chapter on mothering, 'Mothers and sons'.)

FATHER TAKING AN OVERVIEW OF THE SITUATION

Dork dads

You might be alarmed to know that a fair few men actually *don't occupy an adult place in the family.* However hard they work in their job, or however much respect they may command in the big world, when they arrive home some men turn into one of the kids. What a drag for their partners!

Dork dads are especially evident when the time comes to discipline the kids. Their valiant spouse is attempting to get junior to clean up after himself in the kitchen, and in comes the dad.

'Why are you picking on him now?' or 'He just forgot, don't be so hard on him!'. These are fatal mistakes for a man to make. It's fine for partners to have different views on discipline, but you should sort it out privately away from the kids. Men who undermine their partners will have a terrible sex life. (I just want to point out that connection!)

It's a worry how low we have sunk, us guys – or at least some of us. If you listen to some women talking when there are no men around, it gives you a bit of a jolt. They will say things like, 'Sure, I've got four kids, and one of them is my husband!', followed by a kind of sad laugh. Women don't want another child for a husband, they want a man. Not a macho tower of strength, just someone who will stand beside them and help work things out. Women long for this in a partner, and men who provide it are much appreciated.

Do I have to have all the answers?

It was an enormous relief for me to find that I didn't always have to know what to do as a father. As our kids reach new ages and create new challenges, we inevitably lose the plot at times. 'Can they stay at their new friend's place overnight?' 'Is that book suitable for them to read?' 'What is a fair consequence for this misbehaviour?' Sometimes it's a real close call.

What to do? If you don't have an answer on the spot, then it's okay to stall. The best thing to do is simply talk it over with your partner or a friend. If you are both stuck, talk it over with other parents. My kids know if they hassle me I am more likely to give an unfavourable decision, so they have become more careful! But if I genuinely don't know what to do or say, I say, 'Well, I'm not happy about it, but I'll sleep on it and we'll talk some more tomorrow.' As long as you *always* follow up, then this response works well. Family life is a 'work in progress'.

LETTER FROM A FATHER

Dear Steve,

We have had many challenges with our son, and he with us! I'm pleased to say that things are going well for him. Other parents of boys might like to share some things we have learned.

The biggest difference between Matt and his sister Sophie was that Matt was very impulsive and had explosive energy. When he was eight, he ran straight out in front of a car without even pausing to look. Luckily the driver had seen Matt's ball roll onto the road and was already braking hard! The car just missed him. Boys don't seem to always think before they act.

We really got it wrong with Matt in his early teens. Because his sister had been so easy to negotiate with, we assumed he would be the same. But he just didn't do his housework, his homework or keep to agreements about when he would be in. Reasoning wasn't enough with him – until we realised he was crying out for firm boundaries and *enforced* consequences. We had been threatening him, sure, but just not carrying out consequences. When we finally did this consistently (feeling pretty mean sometimes) then he improved out of sight. The thing was, he was happier, too. I think some boys just need this.

Something that really helped Matt was the peer support scheme. In the last year of primary school he had a younger child to take care of and protect. This gave him a sense of being important and he came home full of stories about his younger charge – how the little boy learned, what he got up to. We saw a whole different side to him. Then in his first year of secomdary school, he had an older peer support boy who watched out for him in a bullying situation, so he benefited both ways.

Around this time we learned that although he was ratty at home, the teachers thought he was great at school! So it was ➤

just that he was letting off steam with us. Lots of parents I've talked to recognise this 'school angel–home devil' situation!

At around fourteen and fifteen we felt Matt was drifting into his own world – rarely talking to us, just eating and disappearing, and giving us no insight into his world of school, his friends and so on. Our only communication seemed to be in telling him off. Luckily we always eat dinner together at the table, and this was the one time we got to talk. We resolved to have more time together – father and son weekends away. My wife decided to get out of the negative cycle and to give compliments to Matt, not just criticisms. He responded quite warmly. I think we had just got caught in a negative pattern. Boys do want to be friends, they don't want to live in their own world, which is often quite lonely.

We both benefited from a P.E.T. course. The best things we learned were: use 'I messages' (like 'I was scared when you didn't come home at the agreed time. I need you to make agreements you can keep.') instead of 'You are unreliable and useless! You had better come home or else!'; also how to listen to kids' problems, so they can talk them over, instead of jumping in with advice.

We are a lot happier now, and Matt is a sociable and pleasant young man, instead of a surly boy. It's important never to give up with your kids. Keep learning and getting help if you are stuck. You can always improve things if you try. Kids really need you to keep communicating with them.

Geoff H.

Your kids don't have to like it

It's okay to be unpopular with your kids once or twice a day! If you have lots of good time together and a long history of care and involvement to draw on, then you have goodwill saved up like money in the bank. A good friend of mine (who puts in a lot of time with his kids) told me how he 'lost it' with his twelve-year-old son recently and sent him off to his bedroom, yelling at him as he went. The son deserved some of it, but the yelling was louder than was necessary – the result of a long, frustrating day at work. Ten minutes later, the boy walked past him on the way to the bathroom (having been reprieved to brush his teeth and get ready for bed). The boy uttered some words which touched the father's heart in a most unforgettable way: 'Why is it so hard to hate you?'

Dads do matter

Many people ask: Do dads matter – can't mothers do it all? The research supporting the importance of dads is overwhelming. Boys with absent fathers are statistically more likely to be violent, get hurt, get into trouble, do poorly in schools and be members of teenage gangs in adolescence.

Fatherless daughters are more likely to have low self-esteem, to have sex before they really want to, get pregnant, be assaulted and not continue their schooling. Families without men are usually poorer, and children of these families are likely to move downwards on the socio-economic ladder. Is that enough to convince you?

Fathering is the best thing you are ever likely to do – for your own satisfaction and joy, and for its effect on the future of other human beings. And it's good fun.

In a nutshell

1 Make the time to be a dad. In society today, men are often little more than work-machines. You have to fight to be a real father to your kids.

2 Be active with your children – talk, play, make things, go on trips together. Take every chance you can to interact.

3 Sometimes **A**(attention) **Deficit Disorder** is actually **D**(dad) **Deficit Disorder**.

4 Share the discipline with your partner. Often your son will respond more easily to you – not from fear, but from respect and wanting to please you. Don't hit or frighten boys – it just makes them mean to others.

5 A boy will copy you. He will copy your way of acting towards his mother. He will take on your attitudes (whether you are a racist, a perpetual victim, an optimist or a person who cares about justice, and so on). And he will only be able to show his emotions if you can show yours.

6 Most boys love rough-and-tumble games. Use these for enjoyment and also to teach him self-control, by stopping and setting some rules whenever the game gets too rough.

7 Teach your son to respect women – and to respect himself.

CHAPTER 6

Mothers and sons

[This chapter was co-written with Shaaron Biddulph.]

Remember that first, quiet moment, when your new baby boy was lying in your arms and you got your first real chance to look at him – gazing at his little face and body? For mothers, it sometimes takes a while to dawn on you that you really have a son, a boy – a *male* body grown within your female body. It can feel confusing or even a shock to think that you have created a male being inside yourself!

Most women say they feel more confident with a baby girl. They feel they would intuitively know what to do with her. But a boy! After the birth of a son, it's not unknown for a mother to exclaim in horror, 'I don't know what to *do* with a boy!' However well prepared we are logically, the emotional response is often still, 'Wow! This is unknown territory!'

A MOTHER'S STORY

As soon as my son was out of the toddler stage, I was really strict about him having jobs to do around the house. By six years of age, he was feeding the dog, making his own bed, and drying dishes! By nine he could do laundry, clean the toilet, and cook simple meals. I was determined not to produce a lazy so-and-so like my father had been. In the family I grew up in everyone had to wait on Dad, and I hated that idea. My boys were going to pull their weight!

My second child was a girl, and by the time she was about six, I realised I was much less eager for her to do jobs. The idea was there, but I didn't pursue it with the same energy. I'd teach her how to do things, but couldn't bring myself to keep after her to do them. It dawned on me that, deep down, I just didn't feel good about *making* her work!

When I was a child, my sisters and I had to work hard in our parents' grocery shop. Each night after school, on weekends and holidays, we worked till our legs ached, our feet swelled up and we were dead on our feet. I always resented being *'made'* to work.

Figuring this out made it easier to take a balanced approach. Now both of my children do their housework and have plenty of rest and play, and we are all happy about it.

The mother's background

Right from the start, a woman's own 'male history' has an effect on her mothering. Perhaps needlessly, many people set huge store on what sex a baby is. Every time a mother looks at her baby boy, hears him crying for her or changes his nappy, she is aware that he's male. So, whatever maleness has meant to her will now come into the foreground.

A woman remembers her dad and his fathering of her. She has

the experience of brothers, cousins and the boys she knew at school. And then all the men she has known – lovers, teachers, bosses, doctors, ministers, co-workers and friends. All these are woven into her 'male history', colouring her attitude to this unsuspecting little baby boy!

Her ideas on 'what men are like', 'how men have treated me' and 'what I would want to be different about men' all begin to affect how she acts towards her child.

As if that wasn't enough, her feelings about this baby's father also complicate the picture. As he grows up, does he look like his father? Does that make her love him more? If she is no longer with his father, or there are problems, this can colour her feelings too. A woman may be very aware of all these feelings, or it might be totally unconscious.

How we care for our baby boy

All our earlier attitudes and beliefs about males will be reflected in our everyday care for our boys. Each time we rush to help or hold back to let them do it for themselves; each time we encourage or discourage them; each time we cuddle them warmly or frown at them and walk away. All our responses arise from our internal attitudes towards having a baby – and having a **male** baby.

It's a big help if you adopt a curious attitude – of wanting to learn and understand about a boy's world. As a woman, you cannot know what it's like to be in a male body. If you didn't have brothers (or a dad who was involved) then you have to get more information to find out what is normal in boys. It's good to be able to ask your husband or male friends for information. Sometimes you just need practical knowledge.

LETTER FROM A MOTHER

Dear Steve,

Reading the manuscript of *Raising Boys*, I wanted to add some things I feel so strongly about.

To all the mothers out there – boys *are* different. So persevere in getting to understand and know them. Don't, whatever you do, give up. Or become resigned and join the anti-boy group with their weak jokes and tales of woe, and 'What can I do?' sort of attitudes. There is a meeting point between mothers and sons. It's up to you. It may not be obvious, it may take time and a number of attempts. Struggle is not a sign of failure, but of something new being born. Look for the good in your son. You *will* find it.

Boys have tender feelings, and mothers have an essential part in keeping the child whole. Seeing how affectionate they can be at times makes you love them so much more. Give them a chance to play with and help younger children, and to look after animals. See how loving they can be.

Share your son's passions. Tom (my nine-year-old) and I have a wintertime ritual. On a Saturday afternoon we go to the second half of the local football game (which is about the right amount of time for us) and get in for free. We generally sit down by the fence near the Norths' try line, close enough to feel the earth and air move as they surge past. Tom takes great pleasure in telling me who the players are and the rules, and I notice he often tells me the details he knows will interest me. Something about their lives outside football! The action is great, so vigorous and determined. The atmosphere at the historic ground is friendly and excited, a bubble of warmth on a cold afternoon. So different to watching it on the telly! It's an urban adventure.

Boys often need help in *connecting* with things – a piece of work at school, with using the library, computers, newspapers, encyclopedias. Help them to organise their homework, partition the task into 'do-able' chunks, set realistic goals and help them to get there. Make the task smaller so they can relate to it, so they don't feel overwhelmed and give up. At the same time, don't take over – make sure they have the joy of their own achievement.

Expand your boys' *awareness*. Walking, talking, noticing things, collecting things. Seeing how a tree changes with the seasons, how a building project is developing. Show them how food happens – planning the purchases, choosing the fruit, preparation and enjoyment of new foods. Involve them in planning family events and holidays. Show them how to combine their interests with those of others in a plan.

Make sure they get enough sleep and a balance of social and quiet time. Basic but critical. Bedtime rituals, stories, cuddles, tickling on the back, whatever, to feel safe, loved and at peace. A shared repertoire of favourite stories is invaluable.

Finally, you can really help your sons by supporting their relationship with their father. Fathers may not foresee and plan in the way you do, and this may limit their opportunities to what is nearest at hand. Gentle reminders can be appreciated. Put good men in the path of your son – a groovy music teacher, a valued handyman, a friend's brother. Speak to them about good men, their qualities, and what you notice about how they act in different situations.

Recall their past – tell them what a beautiful baby they were, what their birth meant to you, what a ray of sunshine they are in your life, a deep harmony, a beautiful boy.

With warm wishes

Judi Taylor

LITTLE BOYS' BODIES

Penises and testicles are a bit of a mystery for mothers. Here are some questions mothers commonly ask:

Q: *Should my son have two testicles visible?*
A: By the 'six-week check' that all babies should get from the Child Health sister or doctor, both testicles should be able to be seen.

Q: *Is it okay to touch his penis to wash it?*
A: Of course! You have to wash around the penis and testicles when changing nappies and in the bath. Once out of nappies, a little boy can wash his own penis while you supervise.

Q: *Should I pull back the foreskin to keep his penis really clean?*
A: This is not necessary, in fact it's not a good idea at all. At this age the foreskin is adhered to the end of the penis. Toddlers naturally pull back their foreskin little by little, and at about three or four years of age you will notice that it retracts. At the age of four, you can tell him from time to time in the bath to pull it back and wash around the end of their penis. Show him how to leave the foreskin back until he is dry after a shower, and how to pull the foreskin back when having a wee so as to keep urine from staying underneath it.

Q: *My son pulls and stretches his penis or pushes his finger inside it. Is this okay?*
A: Basically children won't damage themselves, because if it hurts they'll soon stop! Penises are a little fascinating to their owners, feel comforting to hold, and this is fine. Don't make a fuss about it.

Q: *My son often holds onto his penis to stop himself weeing. Is that harmful?*

A: Most boys do this. Girls have strong pelvic muscles which can hold back their wee without anyone knowing they're doing it. Boys are made differently, and can't do this. So if they need to do a wee but are too engrossed in playing, they will often 'hang on'. Encourage them to take a toilet break!

Q: *What name should we call our child's penis?*
A: Call a penis a penis. Don't make up silly names for it.

Q: *When boys are a little older, they sometimes get hit in the testicles during games. What should I do?*
A: Testicles are very sensitive – that's why all the men crouch over in sympathy if someone gets hit in the crotch at a cricket match. But usually there is no lasting damage. Go with your boy to a private spot and check him out gently. If there is severe pain, swelling, bleeding, bruising, or if pain continues to make him cry for a long time, or if he vomits, then get him straight to a doctor. Otherwise just let him sit quietly and recover. If tenderness continues after a few hours, have him checked by a doctor.

If you are in any doubt on these questions, talk to your doctor. It's always best to be on the safe side.

Always encourage children to be careful of each other's bodies. Challenge your son or daughter strongly if they think harming other kids is funny or trivial. Come down hard on games that involve grabbing or hitting people in the genitals. Some TV shows recently have treated these injuries almost as a joke, which they are not – it's just part of the anti-male trend in the media these days. Being hit in the genitals is about as funny as being hit in the breasts, and testicles are far more sensitive.

AT THE SHOPS

Julie and her son Ben, aged eight, were in town to do some supermarket shopping. Just outside the shop they saw two girls from Ben's class at school, sitting on the bench. Ben gave a cheery *'Hi'* to the girls, but instead of saying *'Hi'* back both girls just looked at the ground and giggled!

Julie and Ben finished their shopping and went on down the street. Julie noticed that Ben was rather quiet and asked how he was going? *'Oh, I'm fine,'* said Ben (who, after all, is an Anglo-Saxon male and obliged to say this!).

Julie wasn't put off. *'Did it upset you that those girls just laughed and didn't say hello?'*

'Umm … yes' admitted Ben.

Julie thought for a moment before replying. 'Hmm, well I don't know if it helps, but I remember being an eight year old girl. You did have your favourite boy. But it was kind of awkward. If he spoke to you, especially if you had friends around, you might get embarrassed. So you just might giggle to cover it up. I don't know if that fits here or not.'

Ben didn't say anything, but he seemed to be walking taller all of a sudden!

'Anyhow, it's lucky,' Julie went on, *'that we've forgotten the milk! So we have to go back!'* And before Ben could even gasp she swung round right there on the footpath and headed back to the supermarket.

'You'll get a second chance!' she explained. The girls were still there, and this time they gave their own cheery *'Hi'* and Ben had a conversation with them while his mother searched for the milk – which took a while to find!

Mums help with learning about the opposite sex

As the supermarket story shows, a mother teaches a boy a great deal about life and love. She is invaluable for helping him gain confidence with the opposite sex. She is his 'first love', and needs to be tender, respectful and playful, without wanting to own or dominate his world. As he gets to school age, she encourages and helps him make friends and gives him clues about how to get on well with girls.

You'd have to admit that, in the 1990s, gender relations need all the help they can get. A mother can help her son to relax around girls and women. She can teach him what girls like – they love a boy who can converse, who has a sense of humour, who is considerate, who has his own ideas and opinions, and so on. She can even alert him to the fact that girls can sometimes be mean or thoughtless – that girls are no saints either.

The opposite-sex parent often holds the key to self-esteem for a growing child. Teenage daughters need to have their image of themselves as intelligent and interesting people boosted by their father. He can also teach them to change a wheel, surf the Internet or catch fish. A son whose mother enjoys him as a companion learns that he can be friends with girls comfortably in the years from five to fifteen – before things get overly romantic or sexual.

Giving a good self–image

Many boys become painfully awkward by the time they are in high school. They seem ashamed of being male, of being big and full of hormones. The media continually portrays males as rapists, murderers, or inadequate fools. So a boy may easily feel quite bad about himself as a masculine being.

Mothers can do a lot to overcome this. I've heard beautiful

comments from mothers to their sons: telling them from the age of about ten and upwards, 'Boy, you're a good-looking hunk!' when they try on their new clothes; or, 'The girl who marries you is going to be so lucky', when they do a good job around the house; and 'I really enjoy your company', 'You're interesting to talk to', and 'You have a really great sense of humour'.

Adjusting your mothering to their growing up

As a boy grows from helpless baby to a towering teenager, your parenting style has to adjust with him. To begin with, you're 'the boss' and provide constant supervision. In the school years you teach, monitor and set limits. Later you are a consultant and friend as he makes his own way. You gradually give more and more responsibility and freedom. It's all in the timing. Here are some clues to this.

The primary school years

In the primary school years a lot of gentle steering and helping goes on. Mothers watch their sons' activities for dangers or for getting an imbalance. They set a limit to their TV viewing or computer time, so they get out and get some exercise. (Many schools have banned computer play in lunch breaks because some boys never learn to socialise or interact – skills which they really need.)

Encourage your son to invite friends over, and be kind to and chat with them. Ask them for their points of view and their ideas about school and their lives.

It's okay and important to monitor and check who will be there when they visit a friend's house. Are they well supervised? Boys can get into deep water if no-one looks out for them at this age. They shouldn't be left alone in a house for long, under the age of ten. (This depends a lot on where you live.) Riding bikes around is not good after dark. And under ten, boys are not yet ready for the traffic on main roads. Their peripheral (sideways) vision is not fully developed for judging traffic speeds.

At secondary school

By secondary school, living with a boy is more a matter of fair exchange – 'I'll drive you there if you help me here', 'I'll cook if you clean up'. A boy can have much more separation of his activities and yours. But stay friendly and available so talking can still happen. Be sure to still have special times one-to-one. Stop for a drink and talk on shopping trips. Go out to the cinema together and have time after to talk.

Some boys still love cuddles at this age, while some find it too intrusive. Find ways to show affection that are respectful of his wishes. Sit close on the couch, stroke his head at bedtime, tickle him – find the ways that he doesn't mind.

You may have to make a stand against a school or sport wanting to dominate your kid's life too much. (See 'Homework Hell', p. 134). Allow your son to have a 'health day' once a term – a day off school when he doesn't have to be sick but can be peaceful by himself.

Towards the end of secondary school and the pressure of major exams, help your son to study but take a position that this is not the meaning of life, and that enjoyment and soul-time are also important. Let him know his worth is not measured by exam results.

A kind of competitive madness has developed around major exams such as GCSEs and 'A' Levels. It's portrayed as the make-or-break year of a person's life. We can make a middle road here, encouraging kids to give school their best shot (all through late secondary school) but keeping it in proportion with the real goals of adolescence – which are to find what work you really love to do, while also developing socially and creatively.

Here are some points to consider:

- Kids who get high 'A' Level scores often bomb out at university because they aren't motivated by actual interest in the subjects.
- Courses like medicine are starting to look for more-balanced students who have done other degrees first or had other life experiences. Good exam results don't make good doctors.
- Well-balanced youngsters are happier, healthier and more like-able employees and become more successful in professional careers.
- Other courses and careers (such as teaching, nursing and ecology) often offer happier lifestyles and more human satisfaction than the highly competitive fields like law, medicine and economics.

Learning through consequences

This is the age of building personal responsibility – which has to be learned through consequences. For instance, when he starts secondary school, help your son get organised with books and catching the bus. But once he knows how, after a while, it's up to

him if he takes the wrong book or misses the bus and is late. He'll soon learn!

Discipline works by cooperation. Natural consequences and a sense of fairness are your tools. Negotiate with him. You can't **make** a teenager do things by force – but you provide so many services that your bargaining power is huge!

BOYS IN THE KITCHEN

It's easy to start kids off with a lifetime interest in food preparation, because nature is on your side. Kids love to eat. They love the smells, colour, tastes and even the mess of food!

Babies can sit on the floor in the kitchen rolling oranges around or piling pea pods in and out of a plastic bowl. Toddlers can help you to make play dough (not to eat!), stirring and kneading the mixture, adding bright colouring. Then they can have hours of fun playing with the results.

For four- or five-year-olds, Christmas and party treats are the most motivating cooking (because you get to eat them!). Making chocolate crackles and biscuits and icing a cake are all good kids' activities. Never let them near a stove or hot things on their own though.

Little boys can stir, pour, measure or weigh, peel sweet corn, shell peas, and wash carrots and potatoes in a plastic washbowl. (Growing vegetables in the garden is another great possibility. Radishes grow the fastest. Runner beans, cherry tomatoes and strawberries are good because you can pick more every day.) Boys love to make faces on bread with strips of carrot and celery, sliced tomato and cheese shapes. They also love freezing juice to make their own 'icy poles'. When a little older they can use a peeler safely on vegies to help out at tea-time.

Kids need to be around ten years old before they can use sharp knives, hot liquids or stoves. You should teach them, watch how they go then check that they are still being careful. One child only in the kitchen is a good idea with hot things. ➤

PRACTICAL HELP

MEALS BOYS LIKE TO COOK

- pizzas – buy the bases, and let them add a variety of toppings
- grills – grilled fish fingers, chicken, sausages, chops or tofu
- pancakes and omelettes
- tossed salads
- beefburgers or steak sandwiches with salad
- pasta and bottled sauce
- roast lamb or chicken (See instructions on oven bags)
- stir-fried vegetables and rice
- tuna patties made with instant mashed potato, canned tuna and grated carrot or celery

Be sure to show lots of pride in their work and your appreciation of their help in the kitchen. Show them how they can make a gift (such as a cake or a bag of fresh biscuits) for someone they like.

Don't forget they also need to see their dad working in the kitchen or at the tuckshop at school.

OTHER SAFETY TIPS

Teach your boys to:
- be alert to what gets hot and stays hot during cooking (Use an oven mitt for picking up hot things.)
- handle knives with lots of care
- clean up spilt food straight away (so they won't slip in it!)
- turn saucepan handles to the side of the stove where no-one can bump them or a toddler cannot grab them
- roll up their sleeves and wear an apron (or clothes that won't brush against a hot plate and catch fire)
- wash their hands before they start!

(See 'Notes' for our recommended cookbooks for kids.)

Single mothering: avoiding conflicts that do harm

For a mother on her own, the mid-teens are an important time to renegotiate what is happening. Boys at this age are wanting to test their strength and gain some independence. For a couple, this is easier – a boy can fight with his dad but know his mother still loves him (and vice versa). But if Mum is the only source of love *and* discipline, it takes real care.

Many mothers have told us, 'I have to keep switching to and fro – being hard and soft, hard and soft. It's really tiring'. (Yet it's still better than having a partner who contradicts you and undermines your discipline.) *It's important never to let things get as far as a yelling or hitting match with your son.* At this age, while he is learning to handle his own energies and feelings, he might hurt you and feel terrible afterwards. If you can see a discussion turning into a shouting match or a physical fight, then do the following:

1 Tell him *you* need to calm down. If you can both make a drink, sit down and talk it over rationally, then do that.
2 If you are feeling too angry or upset, tell him that you will come back to the subject later – when you feel less emotional.
3 Go and sit down, or make a drink, or go to another room.
4 Try to act before you are actually 'upset' – if you wait till you are crying or very angry, he will feel guilty and confused.

5 Later in the day, have a talk with him. Set aside the original problem for now. Talk about the issue of being able to get along well in the household and how important that is. Ask if he, too, wants to get along well. Explain that this sometimes involves compromises. The things you **won't** compromise on are those concerning safety, your son keeping agreements he makes, and respecting the rights of others in the family. Ask if he is willing to always stop and calm down if you ask him to do so. Then you can either have a break to celebrate, or talk about the original problem.

By doing something like this, you are saying, in effect, 'For a ➤

PRACTICAL HELP

INTRODUCING A NEW PARTNER

Divorce can be tough on a boy, and if his mother finds a new partner it can also be a big adjustment to make. Care must be taken to minimise pain and increase the chances that the new arrangement will work out. In his book, *The Wonder of Boys* (Torcher, New York), Michael Gurian offers some guidelines for mothers who are remarrying after divorce. Whether or not you agree with these, they are good starting points for consideration.

1 Take care about dating behaviour   A mother shouldn't expose her son to myriad male influences. If she dates, she should do so mostly when the son is away at his dad's place. She should only bring a new man into the boy's life when she's really ready to invest in a long-term attachment.

2 Not displacing dad   The new man should not be seen as a substitute for dad. His role is different. Discipline structures and household routines that are imposed by the stepfather have to be explained clearly to the son and imposed as additions, not substitutes for his father's and mothers' rules and routines.

mother and a teenage son, it's necessary to make some truces, because the situation is delicate.'

If your son is hitting you or intimidating you, then get help from a counsellor and/or the police. A single mother is the main source of love for a boy or girl, and if they hurt or harm you, you will both feel very bad. Yet growing up requires testing limits with someone. Ideally, uncles or adult friends of yours whom the boy trusts may talk to him about treating you with respect. If they can do this without laying a big guilt trip on him, this is great. Hopefully, this is a time when uncles or grandfathers will be spending time with him, so that they may already have his trust and respect.

3 Mending fences with dad   Strengthened by the new relationship, a mother should confront her part in the marriage break-up, mend fences with the father, and include him in plans and arrangements. Both she and the father should rise above any difficult situations between them for the good of the boy. (Except, of course, in those cases where there is danger or where the birth father wants nothing to do with his child.)

4 Supporting living with dad   The mother may, when the son asks for it, let him go and live with his dad. As the boy moves into his teens, she may need to offer this so that the son will feel okay about asking.

5 Your new man is not a competitor   A mother needs to reassure her son that he is irreplaceable in her life. She does this with her time, words and actions, not by buying his approval with gifts or treats.

The golden rules are: keep communicating, keep your family rituals strong, spend time together as parent and child. The greatest gift that parents can give a son in this situation is their own stability.

Sharing a boy with his dad

Many mothers tell me they have realised that they can either help or hinder their boys' relationship with his father. This wonderful letter tells how a mother realised she was 'getting in the way', and how much easier life was when she allowed her husband to share the parenting burdens – and rewards.

Dear Steve

I'm writing this because I thought you would enjoy hearing about the impact of your book, *Manhood*, on our family. It can all be summed up in one particular scene, which still sits so clearly in my mind.

My husband, Joe, and I were sitting at a table outside a restaurant at our usual holiday location on the South Coast. We love to get to the beach for a couple of weeks and take our four boys aged nine to eighteen along with us.

As we were sitting drinking our coffee, I looked over the road and suddenly saw both of our older teenage boys sneaking into the off-licence! When I leaped up to 'deal with them' my husband rose, too, and with an unfamiliar firmness said , 'I'll deal with this'. I was so stunned the best I could offer was a feeble protest. I sat back down and watched him go!

I should explain here that for many years, Joe has been the 'quiet achiever', supporting the family. But in the interpersonal department – handling the boys – I was always the one who did the parenting. Sometimes I found this easy, but sometimes very hard.

I knew that Joe had just finished reading *Manhood*, which I'd brought along on the holiday to read. I wondered if this had something to do with his sudden change of behaviour. When he returned from sorting out the boys, I asked him how he had found the book. (Hoping of course he'd learned all the lessons I intended him to!) His words still ring in my ears. *'Well, mostly I realise I've allowed you to come between*

the boys and me, and I no longer plan to allow that to happen!'

My second reaction (my first was 'Shit, Oh shit, that's not what you were supposed to learn!') was to defend my actions! But almost as soon as I started, I knew he was right. In my efforts to raise these boys to be the sort of men I thought they should be, I had endeavoured to protect them from what I thought would harm them. Sadly, I think eighteen years ago I was right, but what I had failed to acknowledge and trust was that **their dad had grown to be the type of man I wanted them to be and I hadn't noticed.** What a sobering moment.

As I've integrated this learning, I've shared it with other women too. I now believe it's the gap many strong women fall into. **We convince ourselves we are a vital bridge between our husbands and sons, when in fact we have become a barrier.**

This has given me the confidence to stand back and allow their relationships to develop, and develop they have. Our younger boys have especially benefited. I now allow Joe to intervene when we hit the 'you can't make me do it' wall, and continue to be astounded at how effective his intervention is. Not only has this allowed Joe's relationship with the boys to grow, but also a much more mutual respect between us as to what we both offer as parents.

It hasn't been easy for me to stand back, and under pressure I often still revert to old behaviour. The difference is Joe's confidence has grown with practice and he **stands up to me!**

GETTING BOYS TO DO HOUSEWORK!

There are several reasons why housework is very good for boys!

PREPARING THEM FOR INDEPENDENT LIVING

It's not healthy for a boy to go from a mother to a partner in one step. A year or two of independent living is strongly advised. During this time, he will sometimes need to iron and vacuum and prepare something to eat! These skills should be learned during the formative younger years, lest serious learning disabilities like 'kitchen blindness' or 'dyslaundria' begin to develop.

In late teens these skills will play a critical role in other ways too. Housework skills are up there with a sports car in the female-attracting stakes. As a general rule, only cook and clean and tidy for your son if you want him to *stay at home for the rest of your life!*

Even marriage cannot be relied upon to solve your son's domestic problems. The woman (or man) he eventually links up with in this post-modern world may not be inclined to be a household servant to your son. There's a distinct, and frightening possibility that he will have to do his share on a lifelong basis!

SELF–ESTEEM

For a long time people misunderstood self-esteem. It was thought originally to mean appearing on 'Young Talent Time', looking great and having brand-name trainers. The *best* source of self-esteem is actually doing useful things. Being able to cook a meal, iron a shirt, look after a pet, mow enough lawns to buy a computer and hold down a part-time job are all sources of indestructible pride. We should give our kids lots of chances to experience their capabilities.

As a guideline, we suggest teaching your son to prepare a complete evening meal every week by the time he is ten. Perhaps start with pasta and bottled sauce, with a simple dessert. (Don't have boys handling boiling water earlier than nine years of age, as they aren't coordinated enough to do it safely.) Under nine, it's best to leave them to peel, wash, clean, and do other things to help.) Little boys from about five onwards should start setting out the cutlery for meals and finding and folding their clothes from the laundry pile. Seven-year-olds can clear up the table, and so on.

A CHANCE TO GET CLOSE

There's another reason to teach your boys housework on a regular basis, which may surprise you – conversation.

Boys often don't leap into frank and honest discussions of their educational progress, friendship traumas or love life the minute they walk in the door. This has long been a source of frustration to mothers and fathers keen to catch up with their son's life. The reason for this is that males like to talk 'sideways' rather than face to face. They like to be engaged in some useful activity, which takes their attention, while talking to someone working alongside them. This gives them time to search for the right words, and none of that embarrassing eyeball-to-eyeball stuff that women like to engage in. ➤

If you want to get close to your son and help him to offload his worries or share his joys, you have to *do things together*. In modern life, that usually means housework. Whether you are helping your son whip up a delicious soufflé for dinner or teaching him how to get a really good shine on the shower cubicle later that night, these are the times that he will begin to tell you about his problems with maths or the girl who is chasing him. (We know of one family who refuse to buy a dishwasher because they love the conversation at the sink. We think this is madness, but admirable all the same!)

Quite seriously, doing work with your son – teaching him the tricks of doing it well, how to be fast and efficient and happy in making life cleaner and tidier – is a way that a parent and child can enjoy each other, have good long talks and pass on all kinds of wisdom. If you do all the housework for your son, then you miss out and so does he.

Equality of the sexes

Most women are keen to raise their sons and daughters equally. Today's mothers are from a generation that was awakened to male chauvinism and equal rights. We absolutely bristle if we see our sons acting rudely to a girl, and are positively incensed if our son is arrogant or cruel. But we also feel the other side of the coin – a stab of pain if our son is ignored in the school yard, or if he comes home distressed about the humiliation received from the girls in his class or (a few years down the track) the woman in his life.

So we walk this fine line. Affirming him as a person, yet not allowing him to be too full of himself.

In a nutshell

1 Giving birth to a boy brings to the surface how you feel about males in general. Be careful not to land too many prejudices onto this innocent little boy.

2 If you aren't experienced with males (such as through growing up with brothers) then ask men to tell you what it's like being male. Don't be afraid of little boys' bodies!

3 Little boys learn love from their mothers. Be kind and warm, and enjoy them.

4 Teach your boy about girls and how to get along well with them.

5   Praise your son's looks and conversation so he feels good about himself.

6   Adjust your parenting as your son gets older. Keep a close eye on safety and the healthy balance of his life, stepping back more as he gets into his teens, but never losing contact with his world, his concerns and whether he is getting out of his depth.

7   In adolescence, let him learn from the consequences of his actions (or inactions), such as being late for school if he dawdles. This is the age for learning more about responsibility.

8   Encourage an affinity with food preparation from an early age, then enjoy the results.

9   Take care not to have big fights in adolescence, especially if you are a single mother. Calm down, then return to the issue logically.

10 If you are a strong, capable kind of mum, then be careful that you don't displace your husband from being close to the kids or doing his part of the parenting. You and your boys need him involved. Encourage your sons and their father to grow close.

CHAPTER 7

Developing a healthy sexuality

We all want our boys to feel good about their sexuality and able to enjoy it in an intimate, caring and exuberant way. But we also want them to be wide-awake about sex. Added to the perennial risks of unwanted pregnancy and STDs is the lethal new problem of HIV/AIDS. These are very good reasons to want our sons to not take their brains off along with their clothes!

Love is wonderful and often very confusing, too. The simplest and most helpful thing young people need to understand is that there are three kinds of attraction:

liking	is a mind spark – common interests, stimulating;
loving	is a heart connection – warm, intense, melting, gentle;
lusting	is a spicy, hot, hungry aching tingling – you know what I mean!

Young love is a lot to do with sorting out which is which. Mistakes

are inevitable, the trick is to recognise them quickly.

Teenagers (and other slow learners!) fall in love quickly. In adolescence we are often so hungry to be in love that we colour anyone who seems a likely candidate in the bright hues of our imagination. We are 'in love with love' as much as with the actual person. In time, the real person shows through and the fantasy fades. Which could be good – as real people are much more interesting. Or it could be bad – but at least you've found out!

One ethic says it all with sex: never intentionally harm or misuse somebody else. Young people need lots of warmth, positive support and good practical information and a chance to grow up before getting sexually active.

RITE OF PASSAGE

A CEREMONY FOR HONOURING THE START OF ADOLESCENCE, AND GIVING SEXUALITY A POSITIVE START

Authors Don and Jeanne Elium describe a ritual which we thought was a great idea, and adapted it for use in our own family. The Eliums were unhappy that boys often get sexual messages first from the school yard, and that these messages might colour a boy's attitude. They felt they needed to be proactive.

What the Eliums suggest is to set aside a day to celebrate entering adolescence – about ten years of age is a good time. (This may seem a little young, but in our society this is when adolescent pressures begin. It's the time when sexually explicit conversations occur between children at school and often misinformed attitudes are being formed.) Tell your son in advance that you are planning a celebration evening with him. The highlight will be a special meal at a restaurant which he chooses – a real-grown up restaurant, not fast food.

When the day comes, arrange some time for both parents to sit and talk together with him. If you are a single parent, this will still work just fine – in fact, it might be easier. It's a good idea to plan ahead and clarify with each other what you are going to say. (This is not a good time to have an argument!) Now that you are sitting down together, talk to your son about sex, and what it means to you.

Not 'the birds and the bees' (which he should already know about), but the experience of ➤

YOU DID WHAT ?

it – where it fits into your own life. Be as personal as you can. (We certainly found this quite challenging. Our son was a little embarrassed and keen for it to be over, though this is true of any initiatory experience and doesn't mean it's a bad idea.)

Each partner can speak about how they feel about sex. They can pass on the message that sex is great and that their son will enjoy it – from masturbation to begin with, through to later on (*much* later on, mothers tend to emphasise!) enjoying it in a relationship with a partner. (It's worth mentioning here that at this age you don't know if your child is going to be heterosexual, so some light-hearted mention of this would be great to cover all bases!)

You might want to drink some champagne while you are sitting together. Then it's on to celebrate becoming an adolescent. The parents and this child only (no other children) go out for the meal. Your son might like to invite some special adults in his life – friends or relatives – who he would really like to come along too. Have some talk during the second half of the meal about how great it is that he is growing up (but not with a sexual emphasis), and spend some time reminiscing about his younger life and the funny and memorable parts of it. People could bring photos. But mostly it's meant to be just a fun night. It also gives your son a sense of being

special and taking on new responsibilities, and a kind of honouring of him as being no longer just a child. (Some cultures do this at the time of a girl's first period, and girls tell us that although they feel embarrassed, they also find it really special.)

WHEN SEX GOES WRONG: THE CREEP FACTOR

In a suburban council office, three of the senior men crowd into a small office and close the door. The seventeen-year-old receptionist looks up nervously, because this has happened before. The men surround her and begin to make comments on her clothes and inquire, in coarse language, about her sex life. When they finally leave, she collapses into tears.

A young man, a university student, posts a story on the Internet which describes a fantasy about how he captures, sexually assaults and then kills a young woman. The young woman is a real person, a girl in his class, who he names in the story. The police are tipped off and question the young man, but are unsure how to act.

A group of male medical students share a large accommodation facility. They keep a checklist on the kitchen door of the names of the nurses working in a nearby nursing home, and tick them off when someone has managed to 'score' with one of them.

All these men are acting like creeps. 'Creep' is a word we have given to people who act sexually with no feeling for others. They use you and discard you. You'd hope it was rare, yet creepy attitudes are widespread among teenage boys, at least judging from the way they talk. In a changing room, wherever no women are present, the depersonalised and quite ugly way the boys talk about women and girls is unsettling. The larger the group, the more this kind of talk takes place. The odd thing is that most of these boys are actually quite considerate of and respectful to women they know. The talk is just a macho pose. Others may not be joking. The attitudes they express at these times are really how they feel. A big problem is that, since this is the boy-culture where attitudes are being shaped, younger boys in these settings will think this is how they are supposed to talk, feel and behave towards women.

The essential goodness of sex

We want our boys to feel good about being male and about being sexual. But very negative messages come flooding in from the media, especially the news media. A teenager is bound to see TV news about rape camps in Bosnia or paedophiles in the Church. He may read about horrific sex crimes in the paper. For pre-adolescent boys, the feelings must be very unsettling. By thirteen or fourteen most boys have strong sexual feelings and a fascination with the images of women that are presented all around them. The testosterone now surging in their bodies makes their pelvic area tingle and stir. Boys at this age masturbate at least once a day. The sexual energy they carry is enormous. Yet nothing

PRACTICAL HELP

BOYS WHO WANT TO BE GIRLS

A frequent question from parents is about sons who like to dress up as girls or even say they want to be a girl. Alison Soutter, a psychologist with the NSW Department of School Education, carried out a fifteen-year study of three boys in the UK with 'gender identity disorder' – and the news is good.

Alison believes that the wish to be a girl – to dress like a girl and carry out what are normally seen as 'girls'' activities – is quite common among boys. She sees it as a delay in development – not a fixed problem – and one that is best handled with tolerance by parents and some help with avoiding teasing, and so on. It is not connected with homosexuality, and the boys she studied outgrew the 'disorder' by late adolescence.

For a boy to want to be a girl goes against a lot of peer pressure, and so must be quite a strong wish. To suppress this wish seems cruel and likely to cause a lot of tension in the child. In fact, when Alison Soutter went on British radio to talk about her study, a number of transvestite is done to honour this new part of their life. It's often not even discussed. As a result, boys are full of doubts. They wonder if a girl will ever be interested in them, if their intentions are honourable or if they are just another rapist waiting to explode!

Sexual learning includes two parts: the physical details of lovemaking and the much bigger questions of attitudes and values. The practical aspects of sex should be covered in conversations and explanations with your children from toddlerhood onwards. The really potent information about sex is the *attitude* you take to it. This has to come from parents and the adult community. If you don't talk about sex (and right and wrong), they will take their values from friends and TV. Be clear with your boys that there is good sex (respectful, careful about pregnancy or HIV/AIDS) and bad sex (using others selfishly).

men (men who dress as women) phoned in to say that when they were young, they were prevented from dressing as girls and this just made them more determined. It's likely that this opposition led them to becoming fixated as adults on cross-dressing.

Because teasing is such a painful experience and can lead to many other problems, boys with gender identity disorder need help and protection from teasing. For instance, a more 'alternative' school, with more acceptance and tolerance of differences, would be far preferable to a conformist school or one where there is a lot of bullying. Strategies for self-protection from teasing would also be important to learn.

Alison Soutter is unsure about causation, but the three boys in her study all had fathers who had disabilities or illnesses that kept them very passive in the family. It may be the good, warm involvement of a father in family life that works preventively, ensuring that boys find the male role more appealing.

How people get hurt when sex isn't honoured

In my secondary school class (like in every secondary school class since the beginning of time!) there was a girl whose breasts developed bigger and sooner than the other girls. Two boys in our class, who were a little older than the others, would sit at the back of the class and would catcall crudely every time Jeannie walked into the classroom. It became a real obsession with them, and I think we all wished they would stop. Jeannie was quite outgoing up until this time, but you could see her confidence trickle away – they made her life miserable. I wished we had had a strong enough boy-culture to tackle them, tell them to stop, to confront the stupidity and cruelty of it.

In another instance, a good friend of mine at school, Joseph, was Maltese. Because he was a little short, or just because he was a migrant, some of the class took to calling him a 'poofter', and made a game of ducking away from him in the playground, guarding their backsides. Joe became more and more an outsider, and eventually quit school.

When I look back on these times, I feel regret and shame at not speaking up. These days I don't ever let verbal abuse go unchallenged. Youngsters at our house who use racist language or words like 'poofter' get talked to about it and don't do it again.

A lot of boys' 'creep' behaviour is really just stupidity – it isn't really sinister. If adults or wiser boys were around, they would simply say something casual but clear-cut – and stop the abuse. The younger boys would take their cues from this, and the practice would stop. Boy-culture is just the blind leading the blind so much of the time, and behaviour usually sinks to the lowest denominator. Robert Bly calls it a 'sibling society' with no elders.

Peer pressure can work for good as well as bad. Several times in my youth I saw young men speak up and stop rapes from taking place. I have spoken with a number of Vietnam vets about how, during the war, they talked friends out of committing atrocities when overcome with grief or anger. Keeping each other out of trouble is a big part of how men help each other.

It takes skill to steer things in a better direction in a group situation. Kids can only learn these skills if they have seen someone else handling a similar situation well. When I worked in schools, I often noticed that if a child was hurt accidentally in sport one of the bigger boys would be very caring and helpful. At other times the group would just laugh and add humiliation to injury, or be awkward and look away if the child was really distressed. The boys who helped often came from large families where they had kid sisters and brothers and, I guess, were just used to taking a nurturing role. They were more rounded human beings, and good to have around.

A big problem for many boys is the difficulty they have in talking about personal matters with their friends. They miss all the support, clarification and relief that comes from conversations of a deeper kind. In my boyhood no discussion ever went deeper than last night's episode of *Mission Impossible*. Girls, on the other hand, talked things through endlessly. There were many problems we boys could have talked over. The boy I sat next to was often beaten up by his alcoholic father. Another's parents divorced messily during their 'A' Level year. I only learned of these things years later, yet I spent eight hours a day with these boys.

If parents, especially dads, talk to their boys openly, and listen to their sons' problems, there is a better chance that the boys will carry these skills into their peer group. What a difference that would make.

How boys feel about girls

Boys in their mid-teens think that girls are wonderful. They envy the easy way girls laugh and talk with their friends, their 'savvy' and their physical grace. But, above all, they are aware of girls' tantalising sexual promise. Added to this heady brew is a strong romantic streak that many boys have. They can invest an almost spiritual intensity into idealising a particular girl as the epitome of everything noble and pure.

But something gets in the way of everyday relating to real girls. Girls make conversation more easily than boys. It's hard for boys to know what to say to them. And in high school, the girls are much more mature physically than the boys of the same age. They appear like goddesses, to the boys who are mostly little nerds with hollow chests and short legs!

Girls seem to hold all the cards. Many boys (especially the non-athletic, the ill-clad, the boys with big noses or fat or skinny legs) begin to think they aren't ever going to make it with a girl. They feel destined to be losers in the romantic stakes. This sits very heavily on their minds.

In fact, unbeknownst to the boys, the girls, too, are often feeling uncertain and awkward. They would actually like to talk, mix and share affection with the boys. If the boys were a little more socially skilled or bolder, many more affirming things could happen between the genders. Instead, the girls whisper to each other and mock the boys, the boys harass and rubbish the girls, and the quiet ones stand back from it all and just brood.

It's at this stage that a 'creep' mentality often sets in. ('If I can't meet girls as equals, I'll have to control them' mentality.) This isn't helped by the phenomena of the girlie magazine and the soft-porn style in music video-clips on TV. The 'look-but-don't-touch' message is just a huge tease. This, deep down, feeds a strong, sexually charged and (in some ways) quite valid anger. If boys don't get much chance to talk and share with real girls, the more likely they are to start to fantasise about control and domination. Their attitude to women, and their ability to relate to girls as people, just gets worse.

The Men's Movement shares with the Women's Movement an anger at the use of images in advertising which grab our sons by the penis, so to speak. Several years ago, a young man in Adelaide, Australia jumped onto the stage during an Elle McPherson appearance and called out, 'You whore!', before being evicted by security guards. He then went and threw himself to his death from a high building.

Somehow, in all the use of sexuality in advertising, there is a lack of heart. A young man's heart is not unconnected from his pelvis but, as one young man wrote, 'the pictures never love you back'. Parents are angered by the manipulation – not because they dislike sexuality but because it is such an easy hook for lonely youngsters. (Perhaps it's time to get out the spray cans again.)

The end point of this 'creepification' process is the young man who rapes a girl, or the adult who sexually assaults his own children, or the man who visits brothels obsessively. All of these are far too common.

A great many otherwise well-adjusted men carry from boyhood a huge inferiority complex in the area of sex and romance. It makes them poor lovers, and their wives may soon lose interest. This makes the men desperate for sex, being desperate makes them unlovable and being unlovable makes them desperate all over again. I suspect this is the cause of most marriage break-ups. Boyhood is the time when some positive words, some affection and some honour from parents and friends can make all the difference to a boy's long-term happiness.

How boys shut down their bodies

Have you noticed the way that boys begin shutting down their feelings once they reach school age? Little boys are full of feelings and energies. But in the jungle of the school yard they soon grow ashamed of useful and healthy emotions like sadness, fear or tenderness. To make himself cope, a boy hardens his feelings and tenses his body. If you touch the shoulders of a ten-year-old boy, you will often find that his muscles are rock-hard with tension.

Then, one day, puberty strikes. In a shut-down body, one part suddenly springs to life like a crocus through the frozen soil! The boy is suddenly aware of a wonderful feeling of aliveness, of quickening – all located in the one place! It's no wonder that a boy soon attaches all his feelings of closeness (and all his sense of aliveness and wellbeing) to the activities of his penis.

Boys want to feel alive in their bodies. That's why they like music with a heavy beat, and why they love activity, speed and danger. They instinctively know this can help them break through into manhood. A boy who enjoys his body and can hug his mum, dad and sisters, often has many ways to feel good – dancing, drumming or playing sport for the buzz of the game itself. For these boys, sex carries a little less weight – it's a pleasure, rather than an obsession.

Keeping things open and positive

Parents must be careful not to drive sexuality underground by ridiculing their son about sex or girls. Do talk about it when it comes up in movies or TV or discussions at the table. As boys pass the age of ten, use sexual words casually and normally in conversation – masturbation, lovemaking, orgasm, as well as the darker ones, such as rape and incest. Be more open about sex as a lovely and exciting aspect of life.

Demand maturity – with good humour. If you notice your sons sniggering or reacting in a silly way to an incident on TV or in the conversation, don't just let it go – ask them about it, and fill out their understanding. But end with a joke or a laugh. Give things a more positive spin. The antidote to 'creepiness' is an infusion of warmth, humour and openness.

Mothers can really help here. If a mother is affectionate, praises her son's attractiveness (without flirting with him), and if his father shows respect for the mother (and expresses his attraction in a positive and non-sleazy way), then the boy learns how to relate to girls with attraction and *equality*. If boys and girls are encouraged in school or youth groups to talk and mix and have friendships that are not 'dates', they can learn more about the opposite sex without the self-consciousness of 'going steady'. They can graduate in friendship first and major in romance later.

A steady and unhealthy trend towards sexualising children has developed in recent years – in 'sexy' clothing styles, advertising and role-models in movies. Children are the losers in this. Avoid casting kids' friendships in terms of 'she's your girlfriend – how cute', especially when the children are only five years old!

Tenderness is taught

In the 1960s, anthropologist James Prescott carried out a very large scale study of child-rearing and violence across different societies. He found that those societies which gave less touching and affection to young children had by far the most violence amongst adults. It's clear that the more tender and warm are the lives of children, the safer and more loving they will be as adults. (Sex offenders and other sexual predators almost always have a history of rejection, institutionalisation and disrupted childhoods.) Treating children with warmth and affection immunises them against the wish or need to harm others.

Some practicalities: masturbation and pornography

Scottish comedian, Billy Connolly, famous for his frankness, says the following about masturbation:

> The one advantage masturbation has over sex is that you don't have to look your best.
>
> I remember my first sexual experience as a very frightening experience – it was dark and I was alone!
>
> You know, I've always been pro-masturbation. It's the only exercise some of us get. I have to do it to get my heart started of a morning.

All males masturbate, in their teens, during marriage and in old age. It's a simple mechanism for keeping sperm renewed and having a good time. But it's something more than this. Just as lovemaking is so much more than just a physical thing, so masturbation is a way that young people get to feel good and learn about themselves. Orgasm (experienced without guilt in a relaxed and trusting state of mind) is really a spiritual experience. For a few seconds your body is lost in the stars and nature's rhythms take over – and all just an arm's length away!

Parents need only to:

1 let boys know masturbation is okay; and
2 respect the privacy of boys' bedrooms after lights out – and ask that they use tissues to avoid gumming up acres of sheets, pyjamas and pillowcases!

Pornography is a slightly more complicated question. A father once asked me: 'My son is fourteen. He has pictures of naked women all over his bedroom walls. Is this okay?' (I love these questions!)

SB: 'How do you feel about it?'

Him: 'I'm not real comfortable about it.'

SB: 'And your wife – how does she feel?'

Him: 'She hates them.'

SB: 'Uh huh. I think both your feelings are important to listen to. It isn't wrong for women to show their bodies, or for boys to be interested in looking at them or fantasising about them. What's a problem is where and when and with whom. If a boy has magazines, he should keep them privately to himself. His mother (or sister) shouldn't have to see the pictures glaring out. And if she objects to him even owning them, then that is fine. A father should support her in this.'

I posed this question on a fathers' Internet chat group, and there were some wonderful replies. Most men remembered hoarding pictures or magazines when they were about this age. But they also noted that the pictures were far less explicit than now, and not as readily available. Far more was left to the imagination.

The age of the boy made a big difference. Most fathers took a totally different view about boys under thirteen or so having access to sexually posed pictures of women. They felt that it prematurely sexualised the boys, and got in the way of the *real* goal at this age, which was for them to have friendships with girls without being hung-up about sex (for which they were not emotionally or physically ready).

One man wrote: 'I would ask a fourteen-year-old to hide his magazines and keep them out of sight, or I would have to take them. But with a nine-year-old I would take them away and toss them out – and have a talk with him about why.'

Prohibition doesn't work – boys will see these images in magazines being passed around among friends or on the Internet. What is needed is close enough monitoring by parents so that you are able to prevent really objectionable material circulating amongst boys, while at the same time not shaming the boys for being interested or curious.

Pornography can have an educational role, and boys' curiosity is healthy and natural. Boys want to see what women look like. They want to see what goes where, and how! The bestseller, *The Joy of Sex*, succeeded because it was the first mass market publication with images that were tasteful, erotic and quite tender.

When boys do see these images, you can help them to think about the messages the pictures send, why they are sold, what is portrayed and whether or not they are respectful of women. (Some pictures are and some are not.) Fathers or mothers may well help their sons find better erotica to look at and read. It's a delicate but not impossible area to navigate. Keep your sense of humour handy.

Boys may be more obsessed with images if they are not used to nakedness. If they have routinely seen their mum and dad in the shower or bathroom naked, they will attach less importance to nakedness – and also see women as people with attractive bodies, not just objects to lust after. What we want our boys to think when they see an attractive woman is that she is attractive *and* a person with feelings. Too much pornography tends to take away the personhood of women.

There are cases of men preferring masturbation with magazines to sex with their partners. Pictures are 'non-relational', and for shy or awkward men may have an addictive quality. It's a matter of balance.

Parents must also teach daughters not to misuse their physical appeal to exploit or tease boys – for creepiness can work both ways. Sex is about mutual respect and mutual enjoyment. It's a part of loving, and not a marketing tool.

What if your son is gay?

Even before our children are born, we have their lives mapped out for them! And what conservative dreams they are – a career, marriage and grandchildren to sit on our knee! Finding out that your teenage son is gay demolishes several of these fond hopes and replaces them with scary images instead. It's natural to feel some grief and concern.

Part of the problem is the stereotypes. While Gay Pride has done great things for homosexuals, it hasn't helped the fantasies of mums and dads in the suburbs! And it's hardly a realistic depiction of gay life.

When it's all boiled down, the concerns of parents of a gay son are just the same as those of any parent. You want your son to have a happy life. You hope that he will handle his sexuality in a responsible and self-respecting way. And you hope that he will not move away into worlds that are beyond your reach or understanding.

Teenage gay children need our support. There is no doubt they are at risk – from our rejection and from a harsh world. It's now believed that many youth suicides are actually caused by youngsters discovering they are gay. Gay kids need parents who will listen and understand, and protect them from harassment or persecution.

It's not very fruitful to dwell on 'why' or 'where did we go wrong?' Evidence is mounting that some babies are born with certain hormonal settings from early in the womb, which may set the brain as either gay, bisexual or heterosexual. (At least one in twenty young men is gay or bisexual.)

Sometimes family dynamics play a part – certainly some gay men had remote and critical fathers, and are seeking fatherly affection from a gay lover. But this alone isn't enough to determine sexual orientation. Trying to talk a young man out of being gay just makes them feel more rejected and more desperate.

Gay life certainly has its sleazy side, often born of loneliness and rejection. But if you love and support your son, he will be less likely to drop into self-loathing or despair, and more likely to be self-respecting and careful about safe sex, for example.) There are many happy and successful gay men and women. Life will be better for gay teenagers when gay adults are more visible. Perhaps one day schools will deliberately have some gay staff members so that children will see that normal, caring and happy people can be lesbian or gay.

The hardest thing about having a gay son can be the way it isolates you – you feel different from other parents. Talking to other parents of gay offspring is the very best thing you can do. (Groups such as PFLAG – Parents and Friends of Lesbians and Gays – exist in some centres and offer support.) A gay son can take you into a world of interesting and wonderful people!

In a nutshell

1 Teach boys about the difference between liking, loving and lusting.

2 Have a small rite of passage when they enter double figures (ten years) and give them some positive messages about sex.

3 Guard against creepiness by teaching your sons to be respectful of all people. Help them to find settings and activities where they can get to know girls as friends.

4 Discourage the trend to sexualise boy–girl relationships under sixteen years of age.

5 Remember that boys, too, want to be loved, not just 'sexed'.

6 Help them keep their bodies alive through dance, drumming, music, massage and so on. Continue to hug and give back-rubs to your sons as long as they are comfortable with it.

7 Tenderness is learned by receiving it – from babyhood onwards. The real lessons about relationships are learned by age three.

8 Masturbation isn't just harmless, it's good for you.

9 Discourage pornography; discuss it and its messages. Don't shame a boy for his interest, but talk about what is good erotica – respectful,

happy, involving relationships. And perhaps help him find some.

10 Mothers can help sons understand what girls like in young men – kindness, conversation and a sense of fun.

CHAPTER **8**

A revolution in schooling

Many schools today are a battleground. Teachers are overstressed and underpaid; kids have less and less socialisation from home (good manners, calm influences, feeling wanted and loved). The number of men in schools has plummeted. More and more it is women who have to front up to physically intimidating and disrespectful boys. The classroom becomes a battle for survival with only two goals – getting the girls to achieve and getting the boys to behave.

So boys create stress, but they themselves are suffering, too. Girls outperform boys in almost every subject area. Something has to be done about boys' motivation, for everyone's sake.

From what we have already described here about brain differences, hormones and the need for male role-models, it's clear that schools can and must change if they are to become good places for boys. Here are some starting points:

1 A later starting age for boys

The slower development of boys' fine-motor skills, and their cognitive skills generally, suggests they would benefit by starting school later – and so move through school a year after girls of the same age. (Some schools already encourage this and find it very beneficial.)

This needn't be done rigidly. It can be based on some simple screening of fine-motor skills and in consultation with parents and school staff. Many schools today have to dissuade parents whose attitude to education is to see it as a race, and wish to enrol children earlier and earlier as if they can get a head start!

Thoughtful parents will understand the benefits of a delayed start for boys, once these are explained. Since birthdays fall all through the year, the starting age is already a matter of some flexibility, and this can be made more flexible based on actual ability – a far more rational approach. Some slower developing girls may also benefit from a year's delay.

2 More men in school, of the right kind

Because of divorce and single motherhood, up to a third of boys have no father present at home. The six-to-fourteen age range is the period when boys most hunger for male encouragement and example. So it's vital that we get more men into primary school teaching. Not just any men – they have to be the right kind of men.

I have asked many teachers to describe the right kind of man to work with boys. Two qualities come up again and again:

(i) A mixture of warmth and sternness. Someone who obviously enjoys youngsters and gives praise where it is due. A man who doesn't need to be 'one of the boys' but has a slightly gruff, no-nonsense manner! This means that order prevails, and boys can get on with the work, excursion, sport or whatever. But he must have warmth and a sense of humour.

(ii) Undefensiveness. A man who is not only in charge, but does so in a way that doesn't issue a challenge to every testosterone-boosted boy in the room. He doesn't need to prove anything and doesn't feel threatened by youthful exuberance.

One wise woman teacher put it like this:

'Every boy who has been expelled while I was at this school did so in the following way. They got into a fight with a man teacher, who sent for another man teacher, who still just irritated the boy more. It became a battle of wills with no room to back down'.

3 Discipline problems call for our involvement

Boys make trouble to get noticed. In schools all around the world where I have consulted, there is a proven equation: an under-fathered boy equals a discipline problem in school. Under-fathered boys unconsciously want men to be involved and address the problems of their lives, but don't know how to ask. Girls *ask* for help, but boys often just *act* for help.

If we get men teachers involved with under fathered-boys (ideally before they make trouble) then we can turn their lives around. And if boys do get into trouble, men teachers should work with them to guide and help them.

Recent studies have found that boys in school who act as if they don't care, really **do** want to be successful and included. We have just made the slope too steep for them. We punish them, but we don't offer leadership. Leadership is not just something that comes from the podium at assembly. It has to be personal.

Too many timid men and women are in charge of schools. These people have long ago suppressed all their own energy. Boys' vitality is seen as a threat, and to be squashed. The squashing was once done by caning and tedious, grinding work. Now it is done by suspensions, or time-out rooms, or by tedious and bureaucratic 'report' systems. One teacher described to me his school's disciplinary report system as 'lingering, inconclusive, and impersonal'. This is all based on a psychology of distance, not closeness: 'If you're bad, we'll isolate you'. It should be: 'If you need help that badly, we'll get involved with you'.

4 Education with energy

The learning environment of schools seems designed to educate senior citizens, not young people at their most energetic. Everyone is supposed to be quiet, nice and compliant. Excitement doesn't seem to belong in this kind of learning (though many wonderful teachers do manage to bring some fun and energy into their classes, and many children catch this spirit and run with it).

The passivity required by school contradicts everything we know about kids, especially adolescents. Adolescence is the age of passion. Boys (and girls) crave an engaged and intense learning experience, with men and women who challenge them and get to know them personally – and from this specific knowledge of their needs, work with them to shape and extend their intellect, spirit and skills. If kids aren't waking up in the morning saying, 'Wow! School today!' then something is not right.

Some kids are more passionate than others. Their specific passions and talents (not just their testosterone levels) make certain kids itch to do something of significance, something real and socially useful or something really creative. If this vitality is not engaged with, then it turns into misbehaviour and troublemaking.

The passion in the child has to be matched with an equal investment from the parents, teachers or other mentors. The old initiators weren't casual or laid back – they took boys into the wilderness and taught them one-to-one about life-and-death concerns. Their graduation ceremonies were powerful and significant events for the young men. In other cultures boys would dance non-stop all night, or walk 300 kilometres to fetch material for their initiation. These societies understood something about the energies of adolescence.

5 The principal is the key

A male principal or senior teacher is an important, symbolic figure in children's minds. Something between a father-substitute and a god-substitute! Knowing this, he must make it his business to know the kids, especially the high-risk boys and girls, long before they get into trouble. Then, if there's a problem, the relationship is already established and it's easier to talk things through.

A principal is also the key to getting boys to take on leadership, which these days they commonly reject. School principal Peter Ireland wrote in *Boys in Schools* (Finch, Australia) about a strategy which he implemented at the MacKillop Senior College in Australia. Peter began regular schoolyard meetings with selected boys to build up their sense of belonging and participation in the life of the school. The meetings focused on understanding the boys' view of school, the impediments to their involvement, and how to solve these. The boys who participated in these meetings became significantly more involved in both their own studies and the community life of the school. They just needed encouragement.

HELLO HEADMASTER!

(This incident happened at one of Australia's most prestigious schools. The story was sent to me by a parent after I visited the school in the mid-1990s.)

The little boy is scurrying through the school gates. He has been at the school for only a few months. His confidence is growing, but he is still hesitant in many situations. He sees the headmaster coming towards him. The headmaster is king of this domain! A king of the domain is an awe-inspiring figure to a young 'subject'. The little boy gathers his bravery and looks up, a long way up, because the king is very tall.

'Morning sir,' he says.

The king looks down at him and says, 'You are supposed to raise your cap!' and walks on.

A simple incident indeed. And how differently the conversation could have run. If only the headmaster had said 'Good morning! What is your name?' or 'Which class are you in?' or 'How are you enjoying school?' or 'Is your teacher Mr Scully or Miss Plaine?'.

- THE PASSIVITY REQUIRED BY SCHOOL CONTRADICTS EVERYTHING WE KNOW ABOUT KIDS, ESPECIALLY ADOLESCENTS.

They could have had a little exchange. At the end of which, if it really mattered, the headmaster could even have said, 'I've enjoyed meeting you. Next time you greet a master, you have to raise your cap, alright?'

That extra minute would have brought a cheery hello (and a raised cap!) every time the headmaster encountered that small boy. It would have secured the small boy's respect and trust. It would have given him confidence to greet any teacher in the king's domain. It would have made the small boy feel good – feel that he was 'somebody', not just a number in grey socks.

This small boy will grow. One day he may be a head prefect, a winning rower or a grade A student at the school. Or he may grow to be a wonderful man who by his very lifestyle brings pleasure to all who meet him. This single minute would have brought the headmaster knowledge of a boy in his school, and brought the boy knowledge that he had an integral part in that school. It might have set in train positive expectations for his whole school and adult career.

But the opportunity was missed.

• A MALE PRINCIPAL OR SENIOR TEACHER IS AN IMPORTANT, SYMBOLIC FIGURE IN CHILDREN'S MINDS.

HOMEWORK HELL

Men in positions of authority come in for some serious criticism these days – sexist judges, workaholic businessmen who can't relate to their kids, arrogant medical specialists, managers who can't communicate. These important yet emotionally handicapped men all went to school – usually to expensive, private, single-sex schools. Is there something in the pressure these schools exert that makes for unbalanced men? Yes.
This is a letter a mother wrote to me this year:

My son's school is potentially a wonderful school. It has a wealth of facilities, labs, art rooms, auditoriums, sports fields, and so on. It has some exceptional teachers. Boys at the school are winning sporting events, gaining high marks, achieving excellence in music, art and drama.

However, there is something insidious happening at the school, which causes many boys great distress and turns others away from academic pursuits for life. A misdirected emphasis, an imbalance. I refer of course to the academic pressure, and one manifestation – homework.

The school resolutely demands that boys from the age of eight years onwards complete an extremely heavy homework load every night regardless of everything else that is happening in the boy's (and his family's) life. It's so depressing for a parent to hear a Prep boy say he has 'heaps' of homework, and see him dejected and tired instead of happy to face an evening at home. It is devastating to see a fourteen-year-old boy (who has grown an inch in the last ten weeks) trudge home and tearfully say he just can't do any homework tonight. He falls asleep in his clothes, knowing he will have drills and detentions the following day. Are the expectations productive? Would one hour's homework a night give the same results as three hours?

Parents end up supervising and harassing boys who work before dinner and then into the night. Surely it is more logical to set a small amount of homework and teach boys to work on their own. Self-motivated work must be more valuable than work completed in anger and frustration. But will the boy who has tried against all the odds to achieve the three hours of compulsory homework a night give up, lose himself in despair and vow to never pursue a career with university requirements? Worst of all, will he abhor intellectual inquiry ever after?

There are other negative effects that homework has, not only on the boy but on his home too. A boy gets up at 6.30 to leave home by 7.30 for school, and three out of four afternoons gets home at 6.00 or 6.30. He has to have time for dinner. Then it is homework. Shouldn't a boy be expected to take some responsibility for the smooth running of the household in which he lives? But when? It is the mothers who pick up the pieces when the boy is in despair of ever achieving the expectations set. The school is setting a blueprint for many boys – that they will never achieve reward for their effort – and expecting families to wait on boys, with clothes, meals and transport, all to support the superhuman study effort. This conditions boys to expect the same from their spouses – which in the twenty-first century is not going to happen.

When do the boys get to play? Boys should have time to play the way they choose, to pursue their passions, relax and chat outside school. Surely a school should build up the confidence of young boys, give them achievable goals and give them opportunity and encouragement to have fun? Fun can only be had if the boy is relaxed and comfortable in his environment.

It would be to the school's credit if it could take a lead and stand above the destructive values that society has adopted. Take a stand by saying that music is for pleasure and sport is for fun – and that is what this school will teach its boys, so that as adults they will still be playing their musical instruments, still be playing their chosen sports, still debating, still acting in plays, because school made it fun and something they want to take into their adult lives.

Has my son's school got the guts to take a stand? I don't think so.

6 Helping boys with their vulnerable areas

Language and expression are two specific weak areas for boys. As we've explained earlier, boys' brains are wired in a way that makes it harder for them to take feelings and impressions from the right side of their brain and put these into words on the left side. They need extra help to master written language, express themselves verbally and learn to enjoy reading. They have a right to this help under any concept of equity in schooling. Special programmes for boys in English, reading and drama are urgently needed from nursery school upwards. Here is how one school tackled this problem with spectacular results.

THE COTSWOLD EXPERIMENT

Two big debates keep rearing their heads in the world of education, even making it onto the front pages of the newspapers.

The first is about single-sex schools versus coeducation. Are boys and girls better off being separated? Boys not only do poorly at school, but their behaviour often prevents girls and quieter boys from learning. Parents of girls solve the problem by enrolling their daughters in girls-only schools. But where can the boys run to?

The second debate is

about the decline in boys' attainment and participation at school, which has been noted in most industrial countries. Boys are doing poorly in relation to girls, especially in subjects like English, Art, the humanities and languages.

This problem tested the mind of Marion Cox, head of English at The Cotswold School, a coeducational secondary school in the countryside of Leicestershire. Marion decided to conduct an experiment. She assigned boys and girls in the fourth year of secondary school to gender-segregated English classes, where they remained for two years. (In all other subjects, they still studied together in the conventional way.)

As the new, single-sex classes got under way, teachers adjusted the curriculum (e.g.,the choice of books and poems) to make it more interesting for the boys or girls in their class. They were no longer restricted by trying to strike a middle path between the interests of boys and girls. The classes started to take on a distinctly boys' or girls' flavour.   ➤

Class sizes were kept to about twenty-one per class – smaller than the average before the study. In addition, some intensive writing and reading support (encouragement and supervision to read in class time) was introduced for the boys.

THE RESULTS?

The results were impressive. According to national statistics for the United Kingdom, only 9 percent of fourteen-year-old boys nationwide achieve grades in the range of A to C for English. (English is not a subject that boys either like or do well in!) In the Cotswold School, following two years of the new separate classes, 34 percent of boys scored in the A to C range in their final exams. *The school had increased the number of boys in the high scoring range by almost 400 percent*.

And the girls did better too! An impressive 75 percent of girls got scores in the A to C range compared with 46 percent the previous year. (Note that the girls' results were still dramatically higher than the boys!)

The gender separation effects have caused considerable excitement around the UK. Marion Cox told the *Times* newspaper that the benefits went far beyond just English scores. 'Behaviour, concentration and reading levels all improved significantly. I believe if we can catch them even younger than fourteen, before they give up books for TV and the computer, and the anti-heroic role models are entrenched, we would have even better chances of success.'

A GOOD ALTERNATIVE TO SINGLE-SEX SCHOOLS

When I spoke to Marion Cox by phone, she explained that boys at the school found they could relax and express themselves more without girls present, and girls reported the same. She felt that separation 'just for English' was a good alternative to the more extreme solution of single-sex schools. Marion noted that, 'The most frequent observation from visitors to our classes was that the atmosphere was more calm and settled.

Boys were learning to enjoy reading – often for the first time.'

The Cotswold experiment did two things:

- it acknowledged that boys generally have a slower acquisition of language skills, and helped them with this;

- it gave boys a safe environment where they wouldn't feel stupid in front of the girls, who were so much more articulate. The boys didn't have to 'play up' to cover up their inadequacies, and they began to take risks by reading and writing poetry, acting in plays, and so on.

ESSENTIAL SKILLS FOR BOYS

Skills in English are vital to life. The abilities to reason and communicate with language are what makes you a good father, partner and work-mate. Self-expression is also the way out of the terrible emotional isolation that boys and men feel, which may lead to alcoholism, domestic violence or even suicide.

Segregating classes and the curriculum is not risk-free. There is always a danger of reintroducing stereotypes: boys study war; girls study love! A lot depends on the teacher's attitude. The Cotswold results are encouraging: when separated, the girls and boys seemed able to relax and drop the old roles. The boys became more expressive and open; the girls more assertive. It seems to be an approach where everybody wins.

7 Helping boys helps girls too

There is considerable turmoil over gender and education. It is portrayed as being a conflict between helping girls or helping boys. Yet most classroom teachers are not interested in gender politics – they just want to help kids. They are pleased when they can raise girls' horizons, yet they are concerned about boys' needs too.

The boys-versus-girls debate is quite unnecessary. What the Cotswold experiment shows is that everyone can benefit if we tailor programmes to each 'special needs' group in the school. Boys, girls, low-income groups, ethnic groups, and so on all present different challenges. Everyone is human, everyone is special and everyone deserves to be treated according to their individual needs. This is the way forward for schooling.

PRACTICAL HELP

HOW TO SPOT AN UNDER-FATHERED BOY IN SCHOOL

There are four main clues that a boy is seriously under-fathered:

- an aggressive style of relating;
- hyper-masculine behaviour and interests, (guns, muscles, trucks – death!);
- extremely limited repertoire of behaviour (standing around grunting and being 'cool');
- derogatory attitude to women, gays and other minorities.

These traits are familiar to every secondary school teacher in the Western world. Let's examine what is causing them.

The aggressive style of relating is a boy's cover-up for feeling unsure of himself. Lacking praise and respect from older males, he puts on a

- MOST CLASSROOM TEACHERS ARE PLEASED WHEN THEY CAN RAISE GIRLS' HORIZONS, YET THEY ARE CONCERNED ABOUT BOYS' NEEDS TOO.

tough act. The rule is – put down someone else before they put you down. If a boy has little contact with his father or other men, then he doesn't really know how to be a man. He doesn't have the words, the insights into himself or a handle on his feelings. Because he's never seen it done, he doesn't know how to:

- deal with a conflict in a good-humoured way;
- talk to women easily and without being sexist;
- express appreciation or sadness, or to say sorry, and so on.

A boy like this has only two sources from which to draw his image of masculinity – men in the movies and his own peer group. If his hero is Claude van Damme, he may not get a lot of help from this in handling real life. And his peer group is as lost as he is – capable only of   ➤

grunts and one-word exclamations like 'Yo', 'Filthy' and 'Let's get out of here'.

My memory of boyhood, and that of many men I talk to, is of considerable fear of being ridiculed or being beaten up by other boys. Boys dread ridicule – however tough they act. They often feel deeply ashamed of their slowness with reading aloud or looking dumb in the classroom. They dread being shown up by a teacher. Boys who are smart have the opposite problem – being called a nerd, a teacher's pet and also facing ridicule or exclusion. If you are creative or different, you run the risk of being labelled a poofter – or worse!

The boy with good support from his father and mother, uncles and so on can handle this better because he doesn't feel that his maleness is on trial. But a boy who doesn't feel assured of his masculinity has to cover up. The best protection is to act tough and uncaring and radiate aggression, so that nobody thinks you're scared. You get in first and put people down as a matter of course. This way you feel safer.

The same effect takes place with interests. A tough dude has to have tough interests. Boys (not having the perspective of a real man around

to broaden their interests with hobbies, sports or music, or to involve them in creative work in a shed or garden) gravitate to those things that make them feel masculine – action figures with huge muscles, guns, trucks, and so on.

PRAISE IS THE ANTIDOTE

If a father, uncle or older friend praises a boy, this automatically widens that boy's self-image. Imagine the family are coming home from a picnic with friends. The dad says casually, 'You were really good with the little kids, organising that cricket match. They loved it!' The boy drinks this compliment in deep. (His mother could have said the same thing, but in the teens this would not have gone in so deeply.)

A male teacher or a friend sees the boy tapping on the table in a complex rhythm: 'You know, you could be a drummer – that's a really hard rhythm.' Each of these comments boosts the boy's sense of himself. He is less dependent on peer approval and more willing to take risks.

WHAT ARE YOU, A GIRL?

If you don't know what you *are*, then there is one way to firm up your self-image – by declaring what you are *not*. Boys' literacy expert Dr Rex Stoessiger has noticed in his work on boys' literacy that boys who don't have a positive male image define themselves by being *not* girls. So they are *not* everything that they perceive girls to be – soft, talkative, emotional, cooperative, caring and affectionate. They reject every soft quality, and they reject girls too. The gentleness of Aboriginal people, the warmth of southern Europeans or the modest hard-working style of many Asians are all rejected so as to avoid being rejected by peers who are all affecting the same 'yobbo' stance. Having someone to hate and reject makes you feel stronger, more worthy.

Boys' self-esteem is thus the key to ending a lot of racism and sexism, which are significant social problems today.

Bullying

It's a sad fact that getting bullied is a part of many boys' lives. A study of 20,000 primary and secondary school children across Australia found that one in five students were bullied at school at least once a week. Dr Ken Rigby and Dr Phillip Slee, who are leading experts on bullying, believe that schools play a big part in creating the problem and in curing it – but parents can help, too.

Ken Rigby told a recent conference that too many classrooms were based on competition, which leads to less able students feeling excluded and resentful. So bullying was a way for some boys of getting back some dignity. Dr Rigby believes that many schools themselves bully their students, belittling them, making them feel useless, not helping them in a dignified way to learn and change.

My belief is that violent bullies are often hit a lot at home, and have lost the natural reluctance that most children have to causing harm to others. They do to others what is done to them. Bullying is part of a bygone era, in which men hit their wives routinely, and wives and husbands hit children, and so on. Thankfully, familial violence is less and less accepted today.

Ken Rigby recommends that while schools need to have rules about bullying (and that sometimes students have to be excluded from school for the protection of others), a whole-school policy is the best solution. This means teaching in the classroom about bullying, what it is, and that it is not okay. It also includes having adequate staff in the playground and always intervening actively when children report being bullied. The best methods involve not 'bullying the bully' but working with bullies and the group of children so they understand the hurt they are causing, and so make the problem a 'shared concern' of the group.

Surprisingly (to many of us) these approaches are often quite successful. Group discussion methods have a big advantage over punishment in that they don't drive the problem underground or escalate it by making the bully more excluded or more of a social failure.

What parents can do

For parents, the following indicators are warning signs that your child might be getting bullied.

- physical signs (unexplained bruises, scratches, cuts or damage to clothes or belongings)
- stress-caused illnesses (pains, headaches and stomach aches which seem unexplained)
- fearful behaviour (fear of walking to school, going different routes, asking to be driven)
- dropping off in quality of schoolwork
- coming home hungry (perhaps lunch or lunch money is being stolen)
- asking for or stealing money (to pay the bully)
- having few friends
- rarely being invited to parties
- changes in behaviour (withdrawn, stammering, moody, irritable, upset, unhappy, tearful or distressed)
- not eating
- attempting suicide or hinting at suicide
- anxiety (shown by bed-wetting, nail-biting, fearfulness, tics, not sleeping or crying out in sleep)
- refusal to say what is wrong
- giving improbable excuses for any of the above

Of course, there are other possible reasons for many of the above, and you should also get a doctor to check that those physical symptoms do not have another cause. A good doctor can also gently question your child to find out about bullying.

While the above may sound somewhat obvious, the fact is that boys often won't talk about bullying in the first instance because it seems weak to do so. Also they may have been threatened with consequences if they tell, or they might fear it will make things worse to speak up.

If your child is being bullied, talk to the school, be calm and take along written details of what has happened to your child. Expect that two or even three meetings may be necessary to give the school time to investigate and decide what to do. Don't tell them off and leave them to it. It will have to be a joint effort. Either you or a school counsellor can also work with your child to practise assertiveness, giving humorous replies to name-calling, telling bullies 'leave me alone, I don't like it', and acting and sounding determined. In primary school, a boy who knows how to make friends and avoid trouble, and who can speak up for himself, generally is ignored by bullies. Rigby and Slee recommend martial-arts training as a way to build physical confidence and assertiveness for children who are getting victimised a lot.

Avoid schools that are too big and impersonal. The limits to what can function as a caring community are about four hundred pupils in a primary school and six hundred in a secondary school. Anything larger will often become an inefficient education 'factory'. Kids will join gangs for self-protection, and bullying will be a natural side-effect of this.

Schools which are less competitively based, such as the Steiner and other alternative schools, generally have a more caring atmosphere in which children and teachers are closer and more involved, and bullying is uncommon. A very gentle child may benefit from a move to such a school.

Almost every child, boy or girl, will experience bullying and, if helped to acquire assertive skills, will overcome it. Most schools around the country are introducing the methods described here, but perhaps yours needs some encouragement. All of us – families, schools and society – need to learn to live without intimidation of each other.

8 Role-modelling is how humans learn

The role-model concept cannot be emphasised enough – it keeps cropping up with every teacher we talk to. Role-modelling is wired-in as an evolutionary trait in humans. We are an animal that has few instincts and must learn complex skills to survive. By watching a person we admire in action, our brain takes in a cluster of skills, attitudes and values. We don't need our role-models to be great heroes – in some ways it's preferable to simply have people who are accessible and whom we like. An adolescent is a role-seeking missile, and he or she will lock-on to a range of targets before they have downloaded enough material to shape their own identity.

ROLE-SEEKING MISSILE

A role-model has to be seen by the teenager as 'someone like me' or 'someone I could be like'. Girls need role-models at least as much as boys, but girls get far more role-models in school, and those women teachers often seem to share more of themselves. Consequently, girls drink in far more data on how to be a woman than boys do on how to be a man.

• A teacher I was talking to recently illustrated the effect of role-modelling beautifully. In the large country secondary school where she taught, the normally girl-dominated subject of Art had recently become a popular choice for boys, because the new art teacher was a man who had a good personality. He was a father with kids of his own – warm, positive, a bit stern. He was perceived as very 'cool' because he had interests that the kids respected. He organised school football matches, was a keen footballer and liked the great outdoors. The three ingredients – cool, charismatic and male – were unbeatable. He could probably have taught the boys knitting!

The result: a sudden upsurge of boys' painting, sculpture and creativity, which lasted several years after this man left the school.

• 'Being cool' is a subtle thing – for kids are not fooled for long by appearances. To be 'cool' as an adult probably means not trying to be. When I was in high school we got a new, young maths teacher, Mr Clayfoote, who wore jeans and an earring (in 1965!) and drove a green MG (a very cool car in those days). He enjoyed a brief honeymoon period, surrounded by boys in the school ground and being the subject of many girls' fantasies. But it soon wore off, because the kids weren't interested in someone who was just interested in himself. Kids want adults who have something to give them – they want a fairly selfless kind of person. Early in second term, Mr Clayfoote lost his licence, for drink driving, and had to walk to school after that. His role-model status took a bit of a dive.

Role-models can be surprising and diverse. They must also challenge and stretch youngsters' ideas. In the fairly dreary, outer suburban secondary school I attended in the 1960s, I can remember some men who were positive gems:

- A maths teacher who was also our home-group teacher, and visited every child's parents at home (causing a spate of renovation and new wallpapering through the year). The purpose of the visits was to persuade parents to keep us on at school for longer, so we had a chance of 'bettering ourselves' (at a time when staying on for 'A 'Levels was seen as a pretty ambitious thing to do). Although quite a slavedriver in the classroom, this man also took us on the first long school excursion ever – a wonderful experience. He later became a well-known professor of education.

- An elderly man, an old soldier, who taught us to love poetry. He inflicted Shakespeare on us even though it wasn't on the curriculum, but also took us on hikes, taught yoga, and gave up many weekends to take us on hikes and camp-outs.

- A radical communist English teacher, who warned us about the escalating Vietnam war, told us about social advances in Russia, and got us to read *To Kill a Mockingbird* and *Shane*.

- An electronics whiz, who spent lunchtimes with kids who wanted to make and mend radios.

Along with cheerful sports teachers and some great women teachers, too, school really did broaden our horizons on what being male could be about.

A SCHOOL DOING A GREAT JOB WITH BOYS

Staff at Ashfield Boys High School, in Sydney's inner west, wanted to make learning more personal, believing that the closer the relationship between the teacher and the student, the more effective the learning would be.

'We were trying to analyse what was wrong. The boys were not as engaged with learning and were not as successful as they should be,' Ashfield principal Ann King told Jane Figgis in the *Sydney Morning Herald* recently.

So Ashfield restructured its lower secondary school classes in a dramatic way. 'Instead of having ten to thirteen teachers, boys now have a team of five teachers, who not only teach but are responsible for discipline, welfare and parent liaison.'

Sessions have been extended from the usual forty minutes to eighty or one hundred minutes, after it was realised students were having small parcels of learning that were not connected and teachers were not connected.

'We have found it works tremendously well,' Ms King says. 'On many measures we are seeing that they are more actively and successfully engaged in their learning. The real value, however, of teaching teams and students who stay together as a group through the school day, and year, is the potential for the students and their teachers to develop much more solid and collaborative relationships.'

Relationships are the key to middle schooling (eleven to thirteen year olds). 'Students and teachers have to learn to listen to each other, to trust each other, to like each other. They need to be able to challenge each other, but that can only happen when they feel at ease and secure in the relationship,' said Ms King.

What are 'learning difficulties'?

Almost everyone has some brain damage. Small amounts of damage often take place at birth or are caused by blows to the head, genetic impairment, pollution (such as lead from car exhausts) or by parents smoking or drinking during pregnancy. Boys are more prone to brain damage during birth, though the reasons for this are not well understood. Minor brain damage isn't a problem, unless your child has some trouble with learning. In the past many learning problems passed unnoticed because high levels of literacy were less important. Today they can be a real disadvantage – but luckily a lot can be done to help.

There are four main types of learning difficulty and these relate to the way information is processed. For a child to learn, information has to do four things: it has to go into his brain through his sensory nerves, get organised to make sense, be kept there in memory and then be brought out again when needed.

1 **INPUT**   This might mean hearing a teacher properly, being able to understand what is shown to him in a book, or following instructions. Sometimes a parent can be infuriated that a child just isn't 'getting it' – yet it mightn't be the child's fault. Sometimes children literally don't hear or see what we hear or see. Listen to this boy describing his sensory problems:

'I used to hate small shops because my eyesight used to make them look smaller than they actually were. Another trick which my ears played was to change the volume of sounds around me. Sometimes when other kids spoke to me I could scarcely hear them, and sometimes they sounded like bullets. I thought I was going to go deaf.' (Darren White)

2 **ORGANISATION**   This involves adding new information to that you already have. Also sequencing of information. For instance you may read the number 231, but remember it as 213.

3 **MEMORY**   Everyone knows about this one! When you go to get it out again, it's still there! There are both short-term and long-term memory abilities – and sometimes one and not the other is impaired.

4 **OUTPUT**   Can you make sense as you speak, write or draw? The knowledge is in there – can you get it out?

Clearly it's good to get professional help if you suspect your child is having trouble. Many learning difficulties can be overcome or at least minimised. The earlier you act the easier this will be.

David learns to write

Here is an instance of a boy overcoming an output problem – handwriting.

David, aged eight, had a lot of trouble with handwriting. Poor handwriting isn't unusual for boys at this age but David's parents were worried because he hadn't improved at all for two years. They knew that David was a bright child but feared that, because of his poor written work, teachers might think he was dumb.

The normal way to improve handwriting is through lots of practice – practising big swirls and shapes, getting smaller, learning individual letters, gradually building up the skills of easy writing. But David's parents spoke to someone who suggested they try something else as well – occupational therapy.

Kerry Anne Brown, an occupational therapist experienced in children's learning difficulties, agreed to see David for an evaluation. Kerry Anne discovered that David was poorly co-ordinated in his whole upper body, not just in his hands. In fact it was hard for him to write well because he did not sit well or hold his arms in a strong, firm way.

Was this inherited, caused by damage at birth or (later) lack of exercise? Who knows? An occupational therapist's job is to get the body working as best it can, whatever the cause.

David began doing exercises (balance, spinning, trampolining) to strengthen his back muscles and build up coordination of his back, shoulders and arms. This required a six-month programme of about half an hour a day. Luckily, these kind of exercises were quite good fun, and his dad and mum quite enjoyed the exercise time with him. Sometimes the harder parts made David grumpy, but overcoming frustration is part of any new learning. His parents cajoled and humoured him, and kept him going. After about six months, the programme was getting good results and they were able to stop.

Three years later, David still has to 'make himself' write well – relax his body, and really pay attention. But his writing is now good for a boy his age. Although he would rather use a computer to write, he enjoys creative writing and was recently top of his primary school.

Parents make it happen

Learning difficulties require two things – time and resources – and these have to be fought for. Kids whose parents care about them and are willing to spend time with them will always fare better. It takes determination – tracking down specialist help, refusing to be ignored or fobbed off, and pushing the school system to get special help. Be sure to talk to other parents and be proactive until something happens that works for your child.

Resources include special programmes or equipment, specialist teachers, classes or things you can do at home. Meeting other parents whose children have the same problem as your child can be a huge help. It's great to get information and emotional support from people who really understand.

A note of caution: occasionally you may encounter schools that do not want to know about learning-disabled kids. They are more interested in the elite achievers who keep up the school's academic average. A learning-disabled child might actually be pressured to leave or just not be helped. Caring schools will always do their best, and you wouldn't want your child to attend a school that did not care for all its kids anyway.

In a nutshell

Schools can be good places for boys if they do the following.

1 Allow boys to start school one year later than girls, when their fine-motor skills are ready for pencil-and-paper work. (Girls' skills develop more quickly.)

2 Vigorously recruit males (young and mature age) into teaching and also involve more of the right kind of men from the community to provide one-to-one coaching and support.

3 Redesign schooling to be more physical, energetic, concrete and challenging.

4 Target boys' weak areas (literacy especially) with boy-specific intensive language programmes, right from the start of primary school (and have separate English classes in secondary school).

5 Build good personal relationships with boys, through smaller groupings and less teacher changes in secondary school, so as to meet boys' needs for fathering and mentoring.

6 Be alert to the fact that problem behaviour can be a sign of learning difficulties and investigate this as soon as possible.

CHAPTER 9

Boys and sport

Christmas cricket

Every Christmas my wife's family (five sisters, their husbands and children and grandparents, and one or two extras) gathers together from far and wide at one of the family's farms in Tasmania. I love seeing how all the young cousins seem to be instantly at ease again, as if the intervening year since last Christmas simply hadn't happened.

We eat Poppy's vegetables and Nana's cooking, then settle down to a game of cricket in the paddock out the back. I've watched this for twenty years now, since the children could barely hold on to a bat, and have been delighted as the size of the teams grew over the years!

What is most amazing in these once-a-year games is the way that the men, normally quiet guys on the whole, seem to come out of themselves on the cricket pitch. It's a very child-oriented game, so noncompetitive that no-one remembers the score.

A little boy attempts to bat. The men praise and encourage him, visibly leaning closer as if to will him to success. An eight-year-old struggles with overarm bowling, going metres off line, and old men call out 'Good one!' and 'That's better!'. Small hints are whispered. Somebody rushes in to correct a grip. A kid gets out for a duck and is allowed to stay in so he can have a hit.

It's not all peace and light. Two of the ten-year-old boys are at the stage of being obsessed with rules. There is a dispute; a boy yells abuse. His father takes him off to the side for a talking-to. The gist of it is, 'Feelings are important here. It's only a game' – a hard thing for a ten year old to digest. Sport is a lot about character building.

Play goes on. Under the hot sun I am transported back in time, wondering how the older men learned these ways of being with children – a tradition of caring for the young that goes back to the very roots of human history. Sport can be an unbeatable medium for caring, learning and bringing the generations together.

Sport: a two-edged sword

For most boys, sport plays a huge part in their lives. It can do them a lot of good or a lot of harm. It can give them a sense of belonging, character, self-esteem and good health. Or it can cripple them in body, warp them in mind, teach them bad values and lead to a crushing sense of failure.

All through our history human beings have played sport. Even in the Dark Ages, people played early forms of football. Most cultures had running races. The Romans had gladiators and the Greeks had the Olympics. And while not solely a male preserve, sport has drawn boys especially – perhaps as an outlet for their explosive energies and a chance to excel at something of their own.

In Australia, sport is virtually a sacred activity. No religion comes close in its passion, the sheer number of its adherents or its power to inspire. So, for every parent of boys, dealing with sport is a major interest and challenge. Let's look at the pluses first.

Helping men and boys get close

Sport offers a boy a chance to get closer to his father, and to other boys and men, through a common interest they might otherwise lack. Complete strangers can discuss it – including fathers and sons! A number of my men friends have told me – 'If my old man and I couldn't talk about sport, we would have nothing to talk about at all'.

Sport is a way of joining in to the community. As an immigrant child, arriving in Australia in the early sixties, I was immediately asked by the local children: 'What Australian Rules team do you support?' (As if back in Albania, Manchester or Sicily the talk was all about Collingwood and the Swans!)

A safe place to show affection

A friend of mine was once persuaded to join a men's indoor cricket team. He wasn't keen. To use his own words, he expected to be 'bored stupid by macho rubbish'. But he was amazed to find it was nothing like that. The men were incredibly affectionate towards each other. There was real praise for effort, exchange of hints and skills, warmth and (through good-natured teasing) much affirmation of the younger men's energy and skill, and the older men's experience and perspective. The thing which struck my friend was that he knew some of these men in their families and in the business world, **and they were nothing like this anywhere else.** Somehow the structure and rituals of the team allowed each man to be a fuller, happier self. My friend enjoyed the experience immensely.

Lessons for life

Because sport is the main place where men and boys interact, it is often where boys get many of their attitudes and values for life. From a tender age, when they can barely hold a bat or ball, little boys begin to learn many key lessons:

- how to be a good loser (and not cry or punch someone or take the ball away if you lose);
- how to be a good winner (to be modest and not get too 'big-headed' and so avoid ill feeling);

- how to be part of a team (to play cooperatively, recognise your limitations and support others' efforts);
- how to give of your best (training even when you are tired and keeping on trying your hardest);
- how to work for a long-term goal or objective (and making sac-rifices to achieve it);
- how almost everything you do in life improves with practice.

Parents should go to endless trouble so that their kids can play sport. The benefits are clear – fun, fitness and fresh air, character-building, friendship, and a sense of achievement and belonging. And the kids get a lot out of it too!

But quite seriously, the belief that 'sport is a good thing' is increasingly in doubt. Sport is changing and not always for the better. There are hazards to body and mind, and parents have to steer a little more carefully than a generation ago. Let's explore why.

Negative role models and the 'jock' culture

Sport and sporting heroes are an obsession for our whole society. Imagine if someone suggested that we devote the last ten minutes of the evening news to woodwork or stamp collecting! Sport's image is so pervasive that everyone now wears sporting clothes.

We parents want to use the power of sport to make our kids better people. But it can just as easily work the other way. Especially in male sport, impressionable children learn all kinds of unwholesome messages from men who never really grew up.

Where are you most likely to see real-life demonstrations of violence, egotism, bad temper, sexual crudity, alcohol abuse, racism and homophobia? At any sports field! A boy might learn to be courageous and strong by playing rugby or football, and he might also learn to binge drink, be crude and harass women.

Sports' leaders – coaches, trainers, parents and officials – are like elders of the tribe. They should remember that sport is a game, and that it is for the players, not players for the sport (or the sponsor). If sport doesn't better equip our youngsters for real life then we are better off going fishing.

THE COACH FROM HELL!

Fourteen-year-old Jeff was keen on rugby. Because his school didn't field a team for his age-group, his dad took him to a local club that had an under-15s team. This team had made it to the grand final three years in a row, but never quite clinched that final game.

To overcome this, a special coach was hired – an ex-footballer, large and aggressive – to train the forwards. Jeff's father, Marcus, watched from the sidelines as the new coach spoke to the boys one night close to the big match. He was shocked to hear his instructions. 'As soon as you have your first run-in with the other team's players, I want you to hit them hard in the face.'

One of the boys wasn't sure if he'd heard right. 'Is that, uh, if they hit you, do you mean?' he stammered.

'No, you bloody idiot [*the coach talked like this all the time*], you punch them before they get the chance. Understand?'

Marcus felt himself shaking with anger. He had to think this over. This was not his idea of what the sport was about. That night he phoned a friend who also coached rugby. He confirmed that punching was against the rules and could lead to a suspension – and was just plain wrong! ➤

The talent trap

Failure is a problem in sport, but sometimes success can be a problem, too. Few boys today get adequate male attention. If a boy shows promise in football, cricket or tennis then adults suddenly begin to take an interest in him! His father or coach showers him with praise. He begins to move up the sporting ladder. The men are getting a vehicle for their dreams; the boy is getting the approval he craves.

But what if the boy injures himself? What if he reaches his natural limitations? Or the stress makes him use drugs, or he

Marcus realised he had to have it out with the coach. He confronted him – not without trepidation, as the coach was a huge man. The coach dismissed him laughingly: 'Huh, those wimps, they wouldn't do it anyway! I'm just trying to give them some steel, the little pansies. They wouldn't do it!'

So, a coach who doesn't expect his advice to be taken, or embarrassed to be caught out, or showing a slippery double standard? Either way, Jeff's dad decided this wasn't any place for a boy to be learning the rules of life. Father and son talked it over, and Jeff was happy to quit the team. Next year he played at his school, in a team that was coached by a better kind of man.

'Looking back,' Marcus told me later, 'I'd known all along that the team had no spirit – the coaches constantly put the boys down, there was no group feeling, no praise, no socialising or enjoyment. And despite making it to three grand finals, they were always made to feel like failures.'

Jeff's dad was pleased to have seen through to the problem and made his stand.

overtrains? The approval falls away, the older men show their disappointment. Community praise turns to rejection. Thousands of young lives have been destroyed or set back in this way. The more talented a child is, the more important it is that parents guard against 'sports abuse' – using children's sporting success for adult gratification.

How role-modelling works

The nature of youngsters is to take in their role-models and swallow them whole. If a man is a good basketballer, then boys will attempt to imitate not just his sporting prowess but also his morals, his jokes, his attitudes and his lifestyle. (This is the basis of all sponsorship, and the massive global industry around merchandising and sport.)

If schools want to persuade kids not to smoke, to wear condoms or to pick up litter, they get in a sportsman. If a business wants to inspire their sales reps to sell more accounting software (for instance), they get in a yachtsman or a cricketer. It borders on the bizarre, but it is how maleness is measured in our society – and it works. When the whole culture begins to believe that hitting a golf ball makes you a great man then we are in trouble. (We can be sure the Olympics Games will continue to heat up this kind of thinking.)

Think creatively about ways that boys can learn a broader sense of being masculine than just through the muscular kinds of team sports. There are a diversity of ways to be a man. A boy might admire and find tuition from a musician, an artist, a craftsman, a movie-maker or a fly-fisherman.

What about injuries?

Sport is healthy, isn't it? Not according to the figures. Men's health researcher Richard Fletcher found that for some sports it was healthier to stay home and watch TV!

Many top athletes and sportsmen have painful and crippling injuries by the time they are thirty. These range from head injuries through to countless damaged joints and tendons strained by collisions, overtraining or excessive effort during play. Sporting sprains and pains often lead to painful arthritis in midlife. It's becoming clear that certain sports are no longer a good risk for kids.

The real problem is competition. Being over-competitive leads to risk-taking, aggression and going beyond sensible physical limits. *Adults are to blame for this*. Children by and large prefer to have fun; they are not fanatical unless we make them so.

Each year in the UK, thousands of children are seen in accident and emergency departments of hospitals, or have to go to doctors or physiotherapists due to sporting injuries. At least a quarter of these injuries could be classed as serious, involving long-term treatment or hospitalisation. Body-contact sports cause the highest number of injuries, with rugby, football, basketball, cricket and netball topping the list in that order.

Injuries sustained by school children playing sport include sprains, strained muscles, bruising and breaks. There have been a number of deaths of boys playing rugby in recent years, as well as a worrying number of head injuries and spinal injuries. And sports injuries increase with age. On average, between the ages of twelve and sixteen, the injury rate increases *sevenfold*. (Testosterone at work!)

But what if you are not good at sport?

A big problem with sport for children (as it becomes more competitive) is that unless you are talented you fall by the wayside. I loved football as a child. My father took me to a local boys' team but I wasn't one of the 'in-group' and just never got a match. My dad and I didn't know about the boots and bought the wrong kind – Aussie Rules boots. It was humiliating. Apart from playing kick-to-kick at school, I dropped out.

Another problem with sport is parental pressure. If a father is a great sportsman (or thinks he is) then his son may be in trouble if he is born clumsy or non-athletic. A secure and confident dad will be proud of his son if his son becomes a dancer, a painter or a computer whiz. A frustrated dad may be more of a problem. Conversely, a dad who isn't interested in sport is tough for a kid who loves it.

It's important to find the common ground where you can *both* have fun. Don't become a slave to driving kids about to sports you don't enjoy – unless your son really loves it and it feels worthwhile. Look for interests that you both share. Today's father spends much time and money paying for others to coach, train and educate his son. Yet these strangers are often quite indifferent to your child and will give little of themselves. Sometimes it's better to keep looking for that activity that really suits you both. Time spent at the oval with a baseball bat and a softball, going fishing or playing volleyball in the backyard allows for good conversation and the simple pleasure of being together.

Make it good

Right this minute, all round the globe, in every village, town and city, groups of children are wheeling, bounding and soaring into the sky, laughing and shouting with joy, as they play sports and games. For the most part, it's a beautiful part of life. If adults understand sport, enjoy it with their kids, guide their kids into the right attitudes and remember what sport is for, then all will be well.

In a nutshell

1 Sport can have huge benefits for children. It gives exercise, fun, challenges and a sense of achievement. It especially provides a shared interest between fathers and sons, and boys and men generally.

2 Sport is often a great way of building character, learning about life and developing masculinity.

3 Unfortunately, sport is changing for the worse. The culture of some sports encourages negative traits like aggression, egotism, sexual crudity and binge drinking. And 'winning at all costs' is replacing sportsmanship and the pleasure of playing the game for its own sake.

4 When competition and winning are made so important, it is dangerous to be talented, because your life becomes unbalanced. Playing sport too competitively often leads to lifelong injuries.

5 Emphasising competition excludes many kids who are not so talented. Research is finding that more and more boys have stopped playing sport.

6 Sport must be participatory, safe, non-elitist and fun for everyone. Boys need sport. We must not let it be spoiled by commercial forces or immature leadership.

[For much of this chapter I am indebted to the work of Dr Peter West on the importance of sport in boys' lives, and especially to his excellent book about men growing up in Australia from the 1930s to the present: Fathers, Sons, and Lovers. *See 'Notes'.]*

10

A community challenge

The spirit of a boy is too great for just a family to contain, and his horizons are wider than a family can provide for. By mid-teens, a boy wants to leap into his future – but there must be a place for him to leap to, and strong arms to steady him. This means building community links in order to help boys.

If we parents have 'community' around us, then we can trust that other adults, singly or as an organised group, can support our teenagers into a sense of worth and belonging. Without community – networks of committed adults consciously caring for each other's children – then adolescence can actually fail as a stage.

The transition into adulthood takes concerted effort. But how is it done? What are the methods and what is the timetable? What are the key elements? Some are practical: a listening ear, the teaching of skills, the expansion into new horizons of thinking and action, the giving of cautions and protection from danger. Some are more 'magical' and spiritual.

To illustrate, and to give a fitting ending to this book, I have chosen three stories. Each is a story about community action turning boys into men. Each story is very different – a football match, a school on the poor side of town and an island sojourn. Now read on.

Losing, winning and grace

The annual match between Sydney's two most prestigious Catholic schools, St Joseph's College and Riverview, has always taken epic proportions in the minds of those who follow rugby union.

St Joseph's record against all schools is somewhat awesome. It was the kind of record that gave mystical impossibility to the idea of wresting it from them!

1996, however, was different. Riverview knew they had a great team capable of achieving the impossible. So on this day, under a clear blue sky, there was a special sense of history. As the game progressed it became evident to the 15,000 or so parents and Old Boys who gathered to watch that the unthinkable was going to happen – St Joseph's were going to lose the day. Despite valiant attempts by the St Joseph's boys in the last half, clawing their way back up the score table, the Riverview team held the lead. Soon the final siren signalled an end to St Joseph's long reign.

The match was over – the victors punched the air and whooped about. Then something powerful and special began to take place. The losing team formed into a ring on the oval, linked arms and stood as if in prayer – absorbing not so much the loss as something more, perhaps the sense of shared effort, the sheer poignancy of the moment. Then the real magic began. Like an answer from around the stadium, men who had gone to that school, and fathers of the boys, walked towards the circle and wrapped their arms around the ring of boys. Several hundred men ended up in a silent, powerful ring of masculine grace.

People pouring from the stands froze in place and just watched. Losing or winning lost all meaning at the sight of this. It was the sense of union through effort, of giving yourself to something larger – as ancient as the mammoth hunt, the defence of the city, or the thousand other ways men have stood together for **good** reasons. And it was the honouring and welcoming of youth into its glory.

No-one who was in that circle will forget it. Each became more of a man because of that day.

Men at work

A large company in New Zealand was wanting to do something for its local community – nothing altruistic about this, just good business sense. The usual thing might be to endow a youth centre or build a park. They were persuaded by some wise souls to 'adopt a local school' in the run-down neighbourhood where their plant was situated – and to contribute not pounds but time.

Every employee was given the opportunity to go to the school and offer one-to-one coaching to a child who needed help with maths, reading or motor skills. They could do this for two hours a week in work time. The school coordinated the programme, the company donated the manpower and womanpower.

The result was that at-risk children got two visits a week in school time from their own long-term special adult. The effect of the programme was so significant that over two years the school's national testing scores improved markedly. And that was only one outcome – think of the self-esteem, mentoring and the long-term outcomes in turning kids towards positive lifestyles.

What would happen if we took the 'do-gooder' energies of our service clubs and corporations (and so on) and built **human** *contact* instead of, or as well as, chequebook approaches to making kids' lives a little richer? It's hard to know where such an involvement would stop. Getting to know kids in trouble changes your perspective. Benefits flow both ways. Perhaps it would work in an organisation you belong to? This kind of thing *can* change the world.

Initiation

It's autumn on an island off a beautiful coastline in Victoria, Australia. Twelve men, with rucksacks and coats, and nine teenage boys ranging from fourteen to nineteen had jostled onto the ferry two days ago to cross to the island. Now they are awaiting its return to carry them home. Their manner is reflective and serene, like the glassy water around the sheltered landing place.

Seven of the boys are sons of the men; two are boys without fathers. Some of the men are married; a couple are separated. One is a single father.

Yesterday they had walked to a remote shack on the island, where they cooked lunch, explored, played and swam at a wild and windswept beach. At night, they carried coats and walked through the darkness to a place where a fire had been prepared beforehand, and sat down – the boys nervous and joking, wondering what was to happen.

Around the fire, each of the twelve men stood up and spoke about his own life. Some spoke with humour, some were faltering and emotional. After this, each father stood again and spoke on behalf of his own son. He spoke about the qualities of his son, his own special memories and how much he loved this boy. The boys without fathers received this praise equally from one of the men who was there to represent them – adding messages sent from a grandfather and a father in prison.

Fathers openly praising their sons! There was something so unique in this experience that many of the men and boys were wet-eyed in the half light of the flames. Somehow these tears were soothing and sweet – the very opposite of grief or shame.

After the men finished, each boy then spoke for himself in reply (which they did with surprising eloquence) about his life, his values and hopes.

Several men read poems. A special story was told, with ritual elements from Aboriginal and Anglo-Celtic roots combined. They sang songs and had some supper and, in the early hours, walked back to the camp to sleep.

Later that weekend the boys and men split into small groups, talking about the boys' plans for their lives and their goals for the coming year. These goals were announced ritually in a final meeting of the whole group. One boy wanted to go back to school and finish his 'A' Levels, another to get a job, another to stop depending on drugs, several to right wrongs they had committed, one to find a girlfriend and another to 'make it work out with Mum'.

Adults offered support to each young man: somewhere to study; one offered to drive a boy across the country to say sorry to a grandmother he had stolen money from. The group agreed to meet one year later to reaffirm their care for the youngsters.

The stars were coming out in a vast banner above them as the boat made its way back across to the mainland to release them on their separate ways.

Since *Manhood* was published, hundreds of people have asked me for information about initiating youngsters into adulthood. Some cultures – Jewish, Islamic and others – have preserved initiatory and sacred processes for moving boys into manhood. Traditions and folklore are not all lost and may be of great value. While some aspects of our society are in a time of disintegration, all around us are the bits and pieces of wisdom of the many cultures that we come from. We simply have to make our own ways. What will matter most to our boys is that we make the effort.

Appendix

Practical notes on ADD in boys

There is widespread disagreement among professionals about the term Attention Deficit Disorder (ADD). Contrary to what is often implied, ADD has never been shown to be an actual structural, chemical or physical condition, just a set of behaviours which appear more and more especially in boys, and which create huge problems for adults and the boys themselves.

My personal view is that, clearly, these boys and their parents need help – and this should go far beyond just prescribing drugs.

Authorities point out three important things about ADD:

1 The long-term use of powerful drugs such as Ritalin has *not* been proven safe or effective.
2 Much more help must be given to boys (who make up 90 per-cent of cases) in learning calming and concentration skills.
3 ADD does not make children violent, only distractible and jumpy. Violence in children always arises from factors in the home environment.

Be sure that (if you have a suspected ADD child) you eliminate all other possible explanations. Some possibilities are sexual abuse, upset over divorce or violence at home, erratic discipline and learning difficulties at school which make your child feel use-less. If these possibilities are eliminated (with the help of your doctor and the school) and your child is diagnosed with ADD, make sure you and your child get help from psychologists, paedi-atricians and teachers to learn *strategies* to help him concentrate. Just using medication is not enough.

The use of medication can create a window of time for you and the child to calm down and start learning. Please use this time to learn new skills and get more help. ***Don't depend on the drugs to do it all***. Work towards the long-term goal of not needing drugs at all. Several good books deal with this goal. (See 'Notes'.)

Acknowledgements

When I was little, my mother would always talk to me and explain things, and we would go on long walks around the town (I was in the pusher!). Today I make my living with words, and love the wind in my hair. So, thanks Mum.

Dad was good at playing with us – tickling and wrestling. We had a good start in the wet green hills and windy beaches of North Yorkshire.

Australia has been kind to me – friends at school, teachers who cared and employers who gave me a chance to try out new things. While (like most young men) I have known a lot of pain and confusion, there was always someone who showed kindness and turned things around.

I was lucky to meet Shaaron. I'd have been a much lesser parent, therapist and teacher without her. Thank you Shaaron for everything – especially our children.

Judi Taylor has organised my seminars in Sydney as a personal mission, and together we have reached tens of thousands of people. Judi and her husband, Paul, gave great help, input and encouragement with this book.

The Playgroups Association in Australia, TREATS in Hong Kong, Parent Network in England, Joachim Beust in Munich, Marcella Reiter, People Making Books in Melbourne, and many local groups have sponsored wonderful tours and seminars.

Rex Finch is a warm, principled and dynamic publisher, and a long-time friend, and able to work with me in creative ways that improve the results beyond either of us. Dr Peter West, Peter Vogel, Peter Whitcombe, Paul Whyte and Dr Rex Stoessiger all shared their expertise generously, and are pillars of the struggle for men's and boys' emancipation.

We love Paul Stanish's cartoons and Steve Miller's beautiful design. Dr Jenny Harasty was generous with her time and ideas on helping boys communicate. Allison Souter sent great material on Gender Identity Disorder.

Lyn and John Sykes read the manuscript and contributed stories. So did many other people who will recognise themselves but can't be identified.

Thank you to Henrietta Silver, Wanda Whiteley, Megan Slyfield and Natalia Link at Thorsons, for believing in our books and bringing them to the UK.

Steve Biddulph   Winter 1997

Notes

What is it with boys?

Page 2 ' ... boys don't read books any more.': West, Peter, 'Giving Boys a Ray of Hope; Masculinity and Education'. Discussion paper for Gender Equity Taskforce, Australia, February 1995.

Page 2 ' ... they don't join in ... ': Ireland, Peter, 'Nurturing Boys, Developing Skills' in *Boys in Schools*, edited by Rollo Browne and Richard Fletcher, Finch Publishing, 1995, Sydney.

Page 2 'They pretend not to care about anything ... ': Hudson, M., & Carr, L., 'Ending Alienation', in *The Gen,* Department of Education and Training newsletter on gender equity in schools, June 1966. These researchers reported that: 'Perhaps surprisingly, it's the very boys who are always in trouble and appear not to care who most want to succeed. ... [teachers] were staggered to find that those students *did* want to do well at school and saw school achievement as important. One high school took a look at the students who were sent to the "time out" room and found they were nearly all boys, and they all had literacy problems. We found that kids *want to be successful in school* – even the ones who give the impression they don't care. And that message was repeated over and over [in the findings]'.

Page 2 Boys acting unpleasantly: This is not 'a stage they are going through'. Several long-term studies have found it disturbingly easy to predict criminality and drug and drink-driving behaviour by assessing boys as young as six. For instance: 'The way boys act at six years of age is a reliable predictor of whether they will turn into teenage drug and alcohol abusers, say researchers in the US and Canada. Louise Musse of the University of Texas in Houston and Richard Tremblay at the University of Montreal analysed behavioural assessments of over a thousand boys who were followed from the age of six until they were sixteen. Musse and Tremblay report that boys who scored highly for hyperactiveness and fearlessness when aged six were likely to try drugs and get drunk in their early teens. These two measures successfully predict 75 percent of the boys who will later become drug and alcohol abusers, the researchers say. Musse and Tremblay argue that their findings could be used to target younger children in drug education programmes.' From *New Scientist,* 15 February 1997.

Page 2 'three times more likely than girls to die ... from accidents, violence and suicide ...': Fletcher, Richard, *Australian Men and Boys: a picture of health?* Department of Health Studies, University of Newcastle, 1995. Richard Fletcher is the man most responsible for exposing Australia's dreadful record in men's and boys' health. He is at pains to point out that the problem is not a new one, but one that we have been conditioned to accept as normal. It is, nonetheless, an appalling waste of life and health.

The three stages of boyhood

Page 8 ' ... she provides the milk ... ': Breastfeeding of babies provides them with nutrients which especially stimulate brain development. These nutrients are not currently present in formula milks. Children who are breastfed well into the first year of life are measurably more intelligent, as well as having greater immunity. In developing countries, breastmilk is often the only safe means of infant feeding, yet bottlefeeding is often promoted aggressively by powdered-milk companies. This practice leads to over two million infant deaths each year, according to Community Aid Abroad.

Page 8 ' ... mothers like to calm them down.': Phillips, Angela, *The Trouble with Boys,* Pandora, London, 1993.

Page 9 ' ... sense of touch.': The 'finger-touch sensitivity' in human females is many times greater than that of males. The difference is so great that there is no overlap between the genders – the worst female is better than the best male.

Page 9 'Boys grow faster and stronger ... ': At birth boys are longer, heavier and stronger (prone head reaction/grasp reflex). However, female infants are more mature at birth: girls' bones harden and their myelinisation (sheath surrounding nerve fibres) proceeds more quickly in the first few years. Girls reach puberty sooner.

Normally in adulthood a boy will have a body-fat content of 12 percent. His female counterpart will have about 29 percent. His muscle will be more dense and his bones will be significantly stronger to support added weight and stress. He will be 33 percent stronger.

Page 9 ' ... **troubled by separations ...** ': Violato, C., & Russell, C., 'Effects of Nonmaternal Care on Child Development', cited in Cook, Peter, *Early Childcare – Infants and Nations at Risk*, News Weekly Books, Melbourne, 1997. Also see Rafael, Beverly, 'Men and Mental Health'.

Page 9 ' ... **occupy more space.**': Phillips, Angela, *The Trouble with Boys*, Pandora, London, 1993. This is often seen in terms of boys 'dominating' or 'taking over' the space. In fact, this tendency to rush about and make a lot of noise is likely to be an anxiety response on the boys' part. This behaviour is rarely observed in pre-schools (such as Montessori schools) which provide a very structured classroom environment and very concrete activities which boys enjoy.

Page 9 ' ... **girls will notice them ...** ': Miedzian, Myriam, *Boys Will Be Boys – Breaking the link between masculinity and violence*, Virago, London, 1992.

Page 10 ' ... **become a "sad brain".**': University of Washington psychologist Geraldine Dawson found that depressed mothers raised babies with abnormally low levels of brain activity. If the mother rose above her depression to lavish care and energy on the baby, the baby recovered. Also, if the mother recovered before the baby was one year old, then the baby completely recovered. If neither of these things happened, the child acquired a 'sad brain' permanently. Reported in Nash, J.M., 'Fertile Minds', in *Time* magazine, 3 February 1997.

Page 11 ' ... **becoming emotionally shut down** ...': Raphael, B., and Martinek, N., Dept of Psychiatry, University of Queensland, 'Men and Mental Health': report to Carmen Lawrence's First National Men's Health Conference, 1996.

'There is much evidence to suggest that the mental health problems of male children are more extensive than female children and that these patterns will progressively change. Sex-related behavioural dispositions can be clearly identified and these may relate to temperament and to early socially reinforced behaviours, although there is substantial argument as to their biological components.' page 42

'Younger boys have a higher prevalence of mental health problems by approximately 2:1. Boys may be particularly sensitive to the influence of parental and family factors and their interaction with temperament.' page 43

'The boy will also be likely to be adversely affected by school environments which are negative.' page 43

Page 11 ' ... **people to whom they are very special.**': Cook, P., *Early Child Care: infants and nations at risk*, News Weekly Books, Melbourne, 1996. Dr Peter Cook is a psychiatrist who has made a lifelong study of mother–child bonding, and was one of the early pioneers of allowing parents to stay with young children in hospital.

The age of around sixteen months to two years of age is a vulnerable period in a boy's development. A severe emotional separation at this age, from a previously over-involved mother, has been associated with development of sociopathic personality. Brown, M., *Psychodiagnosis in brief*, Huron Valley Institute, Huron, 1977.

Page 11 ' ... **and make lots of noise.**': Gurian, Michael, *The Wonder of Boys*, Tarcher/Putnam, New York, 1996. Gurian's book looks in depth at boys' development, and he has become a leading figure in the US media in speaking about boys' upbringing. He puts more weight than I would on the effects of testosterone, suggesting that it dominates a boy's psychology above all else. In doing this, the author tends not to leave a lot of room for individual variations or overlap between the genders. He advocates smacking boys (not making the connection that this usually makes them more violent). But these cautions aside, he has many good ideas and is worth reading.

Page 12 **The Courage to Raise Good Men**: Silverstein, Olga, & Rashbaum, Beth, *The Courage to Raise Good Men*, Penguin, Melbourne, 1994. A good book, though rather narrowly focused on the one issue of mothers not pulling back from their children emotionally. Australian women do not tend to pull back from their children as sharply as American or British upper-class women do. Silverstein also seems to give little emphasis to the role of fathers.

Page 13 ' ... **rather tense and brittle man.**': this kind of socialisation of males is brilliantly depicted in several films, including *The Remains of the Day* starring Anthony Hopkins and *The Browning Version* with Albert Finney. Both are available on video.

Page 15 'Lighten up: enjoy your kids … ': 'HSC robs young. There's more to life than exam results, Deane warns students' in the *Daily Telegraph*, 10 February 1997, page 17. Australian Governor-General, Sir William Deane, told a parent group:
'It is … essential that schools students and parents keep a proper sense of proportion and pay due regard to the importance of community service, growing political awareness, cultural pursuits, social contacts and the sheer enjoyment of life.'

Page 16 'When boys are short' (study into the affects of human growth hormone) The study, headed by David Sandberg, a professor of paediatric psychiatry at the State University of New York at Buffalo, was published in the journal, *Pediatrics*, cited in *San Francisco Chronicle*, 11, 94, pp. 832-9.

Page 18 'ADD': Jureidini, J., 'Debate: attention deficit disorder', *Australian Doctor*, 11 October 1996. Dr Jureidini is a paediatrician who seriously doubts the validity of ADD as a separate condition. Even Dr Gordon Serfontein, who pioneered the concept of ADD in Australia, writes in his original book that the absence of fathers is a very large component in the problems associated with ADD. He urges fathers to get involved in playing with, and teaching self-control to, their sons.

Page 20 ' … testosterone levels have increased by almost 800 percent!': At birth, testosterone levels are soaring at 250 mg/ml. From five to ten years of age, testosterone levels in the blood are as low as 30 mg/ml. At fifteen, they reach 600 mg/ml, which is the full adult level. From Semple, Michael, 'How to live forever', *Esquire*, September 1993, page 127. Also Dow, S., 'Hormone new hope for flagging males' (the *Age*, 19 May 1995, page 11) reports that testosterone affects the frequency of sexual behaviour; and Dabbs, J.M., 'Testosterone, crime and misbehaviour among male prison inmates' in the *Journal of Personality and Individual Differences* (1995) 18:5, pages 627-633 shows a strong link between testosterone levels and behavioural problems in prisons.

Page 23 Mothers and Sons: Smith, Babette, *Mothers and Sons*, Allen & Unwin, Sydney, 1995, page 20.

Pages 31–2 ' … and thinking about it was discouraged.': (Gender differences are real) Marsh, Colin, *Teaching Studies of Society and Environment*, Prentice Hall, Sydney, 1992. In this widely used textbook for teachers, the author admits that 'biological roles such as sex are inborn and there are clear differences between men and women', yet cautions in the same paragraph that 'it is not wise to emphasise biological imperatives'. In other words, 'it's true but don't tell the kiddies!'. This text also has a somewhat offensive illustration showing a boy student attempting to keep a girl student in a box, from which she is emerging superwoman-like.

It's clear, from some gender-equity material used in schools and in teacher training, that what once might have been acceptable in the name of breaking stereotypes about girls has lead to stigmatisation of boys and a very real sexism against boys in schools. Particularly insidious are boys programmes which are thinly veiled attempts to teach boys that their maleness is not okay, and that the female way of being is naturally better. Society is far from a consensus on this, and parents should be consulted as to whether they wish their children to participate in what are essentially 'degendering' programmes. More seriously still, programmes which target boys from a shaming position, however subtly this is done, could be expected to further increase boys' mental health problems.

We live at an awkward time of transition – when more needs to be done to advance girls, yet boys are being discriminated against quite actively too. Some suggestions from gender-equity groups – such as unisex uniforms for boys and girls – have a lot going for them. In primary school, there is far too much separation on gender lines, between boys and girls, and soon boys and girls stop playing with one another. Everything that can be done to minimise this would be helpful – and wearing the same uniform, queueing together, and so on, all help to keep children being themselves rather than fitting into restricted groupings. One obvious example is that if all children wear shorts, then girls can be as active as boys in play, and so on.

Testosterone!

Page 35 ' … a foetus doesn't start that way !': Donovan, B.T., *Hormones and Human behaviour: The scientific basis of psychiatry*, CUP, Cambridge, 1985. Also Fausto-Sterling, A., *Myths of Gender*, Basic Books, New York, Inc., 1985.

Page 39 ' … a famous study … of monkeys … ': The long-term studies of testosterone levels and hierarchical behaviour in a community of monkeys was carried out by Robert Rose, Department of Psychiatry, Walter Reed Army Institute of Research, Washington; cited in Bahr, Robert, *The Virility Factor,* Longman, New York, 1976.

Page 40 Raising a Son: Elium, D., & Elium, J., *Raising a Son: Parents and the making of a healthy man,* Beyond Words, Oregon, 1992. The Eliums are a down-to-earth couple who wrote this breakthrough book with its very positive view of boys. It is well worth reading, if a little rambling in the style of many US parenting books. It preceded Michael Gurian's better known book, *The Wonder of Boys,* by several years and covers similar ground with a more humanistic tone. Jeanne Elium is a mother who is very experienced with sons, and her voice adds to the book greatly.

Page 41 ' ... do not experience this gender difference ... ': The observation of boys behaving well in Montessori schools was first pointed out by Peter Vogel at the NSW Federation of P & C Association's forum on boys in schools, February 1997. Peter is an activist in boys' education, and edits *Certified Male*, the magazine of the men's movement in Australia.

Page 42 ' ... violent school environments produced more testosterone.': Reported by Dr Rex Stoessiger in Hobart. Personal communication, May 1997.

Page 42 ' ... our jaws and teeth became smaller ... ': Flannery, T., *The Future Eaters*, Reed, Melbourne, 1994. This is a superb book for understanding human prehistory, our place in the environment and what adaptive and maladaptive patterns we bring from the past. It especially focuses on the Australian situation.

Page 45 ' ... being able to sexually assault another human being.': Wyre, R., expert witness, transcripts of the Woods Royal Commission, NSW, 1996. Raymond Wyre is a British specialist in treating sexual abuse offenders. The Woods Royal Commission was set up to investigate police corruption in NSW, Australia, and then extended to cover paedophilia in that state. It resulted in extensive public awareness and exposure of paedophilia in schools, government agencies and the community at large.

Page 48 'The spotted hyenas ... ': Stevens, Jane, 'Hyenas' reported in *Technology Review 1*, February 1995.

Page 48 ' ... "penis at twelve" children ... ': Moir, A. and Jessel, D., *Brainsex*, Mandarin, London, 1989.

Page 48 ' ... Congenital Adrenal Hyperplasia ... ': Moir and Jessel, ibid. *Brain Sex* is a popular treatment of the brain differences between men and women. It is somewhat sweeping in its conclusions, the authors gathering any evidence to support their thesis without always assessing critically. In this, *Brain Sex* is almost a mirror reflection of an opposing book, *The Myth of Gender* by Anne Fausto-Sterling. *The Myth of Gender* gathers every possible evidence to confirm the author's position that there are **no** fixed biological differences between males and females. (Both Moir and Fausto-Sterling are qualified biologists.)

Vines, Gail, *Raging Hormones – Do they control our lives?* Virago Press, London 1993. Vines' book is along similar lines to Fausto-Sterling, but is less extreme. A good typical quote would sum up her position: 'None of this is to deny the reality of brain hormones or the fact that they are brought into play when someone behaves aggressively. The point is that it makes no sense to seek a biological explanation for acts of aggression, in isolation from cultural and social embeddedness of individuals throughout their lifetime'. (page 81) The book is well presented and thorough, and allows of several conclusions other than those arrived at by the author.

The view accepted by most researchers in the field is that biological differences are real, though variable. These differences in turn are affected by how we respond to them. Since the brain is very flexible, especially in young children, we can influence development so that, for instance, boys become good communicators and girls develop mathematical skills, and so on. The either–or argument is no longer given serious consideration; it is the interaction of sex and environment that offers a really interesting avenue forward.

There are real practical consequences which have not yet found their way into education. For instance, the way in which we might make a boy into a good reader is often not the same way that we might use with a girl.

One of the people who has done most thinking in this area is Dr Judith Rapoport, Head of Child Psychiatry at the US National Institute of Mental Health. In answer to the question, 'Is it biology or social influences that have made boys such a problem?', she answers, 'It's both. This is a complex issue because there are several things that are going on that are all true'.

Biology makes boys restless, explosive and searching for leadership and direction. Our society gives them no outlets for this and abandons them to solitude or the peer-group gang. A boy may be going through a difficult adolescence, but because we look on all male energy as being suspect, he is painted into a corner as a bad kid. 'We have to ask if society is more intolerant about males and more ready to label them as medical cases', Rapoport told the *Los Angeles Times*. 'It's possible that aggression and other masculine traits, including many that were once admired, have been so pathologised that today Tom Sawyer would be labelled as disturbed'. D'Antonio, M., 'The Fragile Sex', *Los Angeles Times*, 4 December 1994, page 16.

Page 48 ' ... **excess sensitivity to testosterone ...**': in Leo, John, 'Sex: it's all in your brain'. *U.S. News and World Report*, 27 February 1995, page 22.

Page 49 **Welsh choirs**: in Kimura, D., 'Are men's and women's brains really different?', *Canadian Psychology*, 1987, 28.2, page 133 ff.

Page 49 **Rats licking babies**: Celia Moore and colleagues, cited in Vines, G., *Raging Hormones*, ibid, pages 88-89.

How boys' and girls' brains differ

Page 52 ' ... **gender differences are evident in the unborn baby's brain.**: in Kimura, op cit. 'It is probably true that hormones organise the brain early in life, and also true that we see typically distinct patterns of brain organisation in adult men and women'. Kimura goes on to add that hormones affect performance throughout life, and that handedness and intelligence also influence how the brain is organised. It is more complex than just gender, though gender is a major influence.

Page 52 '**The corpus callosum in boys is proportionately smaller ...**': Neuroanatomist Laura Allen, working at UCLA, found from actual dissection of brains of men and women and children that the corpus callosum is much larger in females. This is the part of the brain that passes information from the logical side of the brain, into the intuitive side, and back again. It may be that this explains how women can manage to express themselves better, especially about subtle or emotional aspects, as well as their ability to remember a shopping list while watching a toddler and talking to a friend in the supermarket.

Men tend to stay in one side of their brain, becoming good at logical or very focused tasks. She told the *Los Angeles Times*: 'It used to be accepted that men and women process information the same way. We now know that this is not true. The entire brain is different at a very subtle level, at least.'

Page 52 ' ... **localised on one part of one side only.**': Bennett, A., Shaywitz, Sally E., 'Sex Differences in the Functional Organization of the Brain for Language', *Nature*, 1995, 373, 607-9. This study represents a turning point. It was the first major cooperation between many disciplines – from radiology, to physics, paediatrics and neurology – to look at the question of differing brain structure using MRI imaging of the brain actually doing thinking tasks. MRI imaging is new, extremely costly and not without risks to the subjects, and so had not often been carried out prior to this study. I have quoted the abstract in full.

'The question of whether there exist sex differences in the functional organization of the brain for language represents an area of considerable debate. A long held, but unconfirmed hypothesis, posits that in general, language functions are more likely to be highly lateralized in males but represented in both cerebral hemispheres in females. Here we use echo-planar functionalmagnetic resonance imaging (fMRI) to study 38 right-handed subjects (19 males and 19 females) during orthographic (letter recognition), phonological (rhyme) and semantic (semantic category) tasks. We find significant sex differences in activation patterns during phonological tasks: in males, brain activation is localized to left inferior frontal gyrus (IFG) regions; in females the pattern of activation is very different, engaging more diffuse neural systems involving both left and right IFG regions. These data provide the first clear evidence of sex differences in the functional organization of the brain for language and indicate that these differences exist at the level of phonological processing.'

Page 54 ' ... **prevent your child having learning or language problems ...**': Harasty, J., Double, K., Halliday, G.M., Kril, J.J., McRitchie, D.A., 'Language Associated Cortical Regions are Proportionally Larger in the Female Brain'. *Archives of Neurology*, October, 1996. 'Our results suggest that women have proportionately larger Wernicke's and Broca's language associated regions compared with men. These anatomical differences may correlate with superior language skills previously demonstrated in women.'

Page 60 ' ... "fine-motor coordination" ...': Vann, A.S., 'Let's not push our kindergarten kids', Vol. 57, *Education Digest*, 9/1/91, page 43 (Courtesy Electric Library). Also, Cratty, B.J., *Perceptual Motor Development in Infants and Children*, Prentice Hall, New Jersey, 1986 (612.65/Crat).

'Sex-related differences in motor development are present as early as the pre-school years. Boys are slightly advanced over girls in abilities that emphasize force and power. Girls have an edge in fine-motor skills of drawing and penmanship and in certain gross-motor capacities that combine balance and foot movement such as hopping and skipping. Girls are ahead of boys in overall physical maturity, which may be partly responsible for their better balance and precision of movement.

'Only in mid–late teens, do boys catch up with girls. At this age, boys increase in speed, strength and endurance athletically, until even the average boy outperforms most girls.'

Hellinck, Walter-Grietens, Hans-al, et, 'Competence and behavioral problems in 6- to 12-year-old children in Flanders (Belgium) and ... ', Vol. 2, *Journal of Emotional & Behavioural Disorders*, 07-01-1994, page 130.

'The typical girl is slightly shorter than the typical boy at all ages until adolescence. She becomes taller shortly after age 11 because her adolescent spurt takes place two years earlier than the boy's. At age 14 she is surpassed again in height by the typical boy, whose adolescent spurt has now started, while hers is nearly finished. In the same way, the typical girl weighs a little less than the boy at birth, equals him at age eight, becomes heavier at age nine or 10, and remains so until about age 14½.

'Girls obtained significantly higher scores on all competence items and sub-scales on which sex differences were found, and also on Total Competence. Sex differences in competence may be a reflection of developmental and maturation differences between boys and girls, particularly in acquiring cognitive and social skills to perform well in school (Berk, 1989; Kogan, 1983; Minuchin & Shapiro, 1983). One could suppose that achievement demands (e.g., school performance) for boys still are higher than achievement demands for girls and that girls' performances are more easily qualified as "sufficient" by parents and teachers than are those of boys. Girls scored higher than boys for non-sports activities.

'No sex differences in standard developmental milestones – sitting up, walking, grasping. Although no sex differences in 5-6 yr olds for vocabulary size, utterance length, grammatical complexity, girls begin talking earlier and language problems occur far more in males (boys outnumber girls in remedial reading classes by 4:1).

'Male foetus more likely to abort, higher rate of congenital defects and anoxia. Greater male vulnerability – shift from female to male developmental pattern increases chances of mishap or females have extra genetic protection with respect to any aspect of development affected by gene on the X chromosome.' Published 29 January, © 1996 Deseret News Publishing Co. Lecture 7: 'Sex or gender?'.

Page 64 More Secrets of Happy Children: Biddulph, Steve, HarperCollins, Sydney, 1994.

What dads can do

Page 66 'In England, ... fathers have increased the time they spend with children ... ': Adrienne Burgess, *Fatherhood Reclaimed*, Vermillion, London, 1997.

Page 70 'If you want to get along with boys, learn to wrestle!: Paul Whyte, Sydney Men's Network, at 'Boys in Education' seminar, Hobart, 1994.

Page 72 The Making of Love: Biddulph, S., and Biddulph, S., *The Making of Love*, Doubleday, Sydney, 1989.

Page 72 'What fathers do': Copyright © 1992 by Jack Kammer. Jack Kammer is also the author of *Good Will Toward Men* (St Martin's Press, New York, 1995).

Page 81 ' ... the importance of dads is overwhelming.': Blankenhorn. D., *Fatherless America*, Basic Books, New York, 1995.
Blankenhorn's book is statistically well researched, and makes a powerful case, especially for the US where 40 percent of children do not have their father in the home. Low attainment at school, teen pregnancy, juvenile crime convictions, learning difficulties and early school leaving, as well as domestic violence and sexual abuse of children, are all higher in families where the birth father is no longer present. His conclusions are less convincing – that we must 'make' fathers be more responsible. He doesn't really understand that men want to be good fathers.

Children ideally need a man and a woman

who are lovingly invested and committed to them. Single mothers can raise children well, lesbian couples can raise children well, but whenever I talk to single mothers or lesbian parents, they are acutely aware of the need for same-sex role-models for their sons, and most take active steps to organise these, against considerable difficulties. Having a real, live father on the spot is clearly the best arrangement if he is a half-reasonable, safe and caring man.

Mothers and sons

Page 89 'Testicles are very sensitive ... ': Acknowledgements to Dr Nick Cooling of the University of Tasmania for verifying and expanding this advice.

Page 96 Cookbooks for kids: Here are our suggestions:
Sunshine Cookery: Healthy Food That's Fun for Kids by Sheila Moloney, Martello Books, ISBN 1 86023 007 5.
Kid's Cook Book, Family Circle Step-by-step Cookery Collection, Murdoch Books, ISBN 0 86411 258 0.
Kitchen Crew: Wholefood Cookery Book by Stephanie Lashford, Ashgrove, ISBN 0 906798 63 9.

Page 98 What to do when you remarry or find a partner: *The Wonder of Boys*, Michael Gurian, Tarcher/Putnam, New York, 1996.

Page 102 'Real self-esteem ... Martin Seligman ... ': Seligman, M., *Learned Optimism*, Random House, Sydney, 1992, page 84.

Developing a healthy sexuality

Page 112 ' ... "gender identity disorder" ... ': Soutter, Allison, 'A longitudinal study of three cases of gender identity disorder of childhood successfully resolved in the school setting'. Published in *School Psychology International*, Vol. 17, 1996, pages 49-57.

Page 114 'Robert Bly calls it a "sibling society" ... ': Bly, Robert, *The Sibling Society*, Heinemann, Australia, 1996.

Page 120 ' ... James Prescott ... child-rearing and violence.': Prescott, J.W., 'Body pleasure and the origins of violence'. *The Futurist*, Bethesda, MD.

Page 120 Billy Connolly: Connolly, Billy, *World Tour of Australia*, BBC Books, London, 1996.

Page 122 The Joy of Sex : Comfort, Alex, *The Joy of Sex*, Quartet Press, London, 1974.

Page 123 ' ... many youth suicides are actually caused by youngsters discovering they are gay.': In 'Being gay is a big factor in youth suicides', Debra Jopson, (*Sydney Morning Herald*, 26 February 1997) referred to the large-scale research of Dr Gary Remafedi at University of Minnesota, which found that 30 percent of gay adolescent boys said they had tried to kill themselves. Risk factors were 'coming out' at an early age, substance abuse and displaying behaviour considered effeminate.

A revolution in schooling

Page 128 'So it's vital we get more men into primary school teaching.': There is clearly a recruitment problem in schools today. Many school principals are quite aware of these needs and compete to attract trained men of the right type, especially in primary schools. Many teachers tell me the problem is teacher training – that they got little in the way of classroom skills or relevant practice from their university courses, and that this lack of skills means they become overwhelmed and repressive in the classroom in order to cope.

And it doesn't help that boys come to school so underfathered they have no self-control or inner calmness, and the teacher's day is spent in crowd control.

The proportion of males choosing classroom teaching as a career, especially in primary schools, is declining drastically. Clearly we have to take steps to bring more men into teaching. Two steps might be: better pay and better training (including accelerated training for mature age entry to encourage men thirty years and over to enter teaching from other careers).

Page 129 'Undefensiveness ... in a way that doesn't issue a challenge ... ': The tendency of men teachers to get 'hormonally' stirred up when teaching boys who threaten them has an amusing and probably comparable parallel in work with primates. 'Adolescent male chimps in the facility test recruits by spitting water, banging on cages and similar stunts. Deborah Fouts reports that women survive the initiation at a rate of 3 to 1 over men because women ignore the antics, just as they would a two-year-old acting out; men tend to be get impatient, react to the provocation, and escalate the chimps' rampages.' Reported inVines, *Raging Hormones*, ibid.

Pages 129–130 'Recent studies have found that ... boys ... really do want to be successful ... ': Hudson & Carr, ibid.

Page 131 Boys in Schools: Ireland, Peter, *Boys in Schools*, Fletcher & Browne, Finch Publishing, Sydney, 1995.

Page 136 ' ... boys' brains are wired in a way ... ': Dunaif-Hattis, J., *Doubling the Brain: on the evolution of brain lateralization and its implications for language*. Cited in *Grolier's Encyclopedia.*

Page 143 ' ... there is one way to firm up your self-image ... ': Stoessiger, R., 'Boys and Literacy – an equity issue'. Accessible at Manhood Online website: http://www.manhood.com.au

Page 145 'What parents can do': Adapted from *Bullying in Schools and What to do About it*, Rigby, Ken, published by ACER, Canberra, 1996.

Page 150 ' ... Ashfield principal Ann King ... ': 'Mid-school Crisis' in *Sydney Morning Herald*, 17 February 1997, page 12.

Page 151 'Listen to this boy describing his sensory problems.': 'What is it like to be autistic?', Darren White, *Autism Spectrum Disorder*, Autistic Association of NSW, Sydney, 1992.

Boys and sport

Page 161 ' ... parents guard against 'sports abuse' ... ': Messner, Michael, *Power at Play: Sports and the problem of masculinity*, Beacon Press, Boston, 1992.

Page 162 Richard Fletcher: Lecture to Men's Health and Wellbeing Association (NSW) Open Day, November 1996, Sydney.

Page 163 ' injuries sustained by school children playing sport...': *Sydney Morning Herald*, Team sports accounted for 75 percent of all sports injuries in Australia. The most dangerous category of sports included rugby league and rugby union. The second most dangerous category included Australian rules football, grass skiing, boxing, ice hockey, parachuting, skateboard riding and snow skiing. The third most dangerous group included hockey and cycling. The fourth included basketball, cricket, gymnastics, netball, soccer, squash and touch football.

Footballers suffered about 54 percent of all knee injuries and 52 percent of all ankle injuries. Ankle injuries were the most common sports injuries. They made up 14 percent of all injuries but only 6 percent of the cost of all injuries. Knee injuries were slightly less common but more expensive because about one in five required surgical treatment. Knee injuries accounted for 12 percent of all injuries but 25 percent of the cost of all injuries.

Page 165 Fathers, Sons and Lovers, West, Peter, Finch Publishing, Sydney, 1996.

Appendix ADD

Page 172 'Authorities point out three important things about ADD.': Report from the National Health and Medical Research Council, November 1996, referred to in 'Pay Attention' by Deborah Smith, *Sydney Morning Herald*, 13 November 1996, page A15.

Page 172 ' ... not needing drugs at all.': A good book on how to do this is *Creating Kids Who Can Concentrate* by Jean Robb and Hilary Letts. See also 'Worries on use of stimulant drugs for children' by Melissa Sweet in the *Sydney Morning Herald*, 1 May 1996.

Index

Parent Network

Would you like support for carrying out some of the ideas in this book? Then you might be interested in attending a course run by Parent Network to help break old patterns and give new strategies for handling the ups and downs of family life.

Parent Network is a national charity founded in 1986 which trains parents to run courses for other parents. Courses include Parent-Link, Understanding Children, Understanding Adolescents and Conflict Management Between Children.

Parents, grandparents and carers from all kinds of backgrounds, cultures and ethnic groups are welcomed.

Our philosophy

Parent Network believes that parenting is the most important job most of us will ever do. Every child and every parent is unique so parenting must be an art rather than a science – and like artists we as parents are constantly learning and can gain from looking at how others do things.

Love is an active verb – a 'doing word' – putting the feeling into practice in the day-to-day round of keeping a family going is hard. Our own children 'wind us up' in ways which we could not have imagined before we had them. Parent Network courses help us to clarify our feelings about how we were brought up – the good things as well as what we disliked. Remembering our own childhoods helps us to understand and empathise with our children.

Our style and approach to running courses is based on ideas of helping everyone to join in, our facilitators are parents themselves and share their own experiences – what worked for them, and what didn't! They also teach skills in listening and assertiveness which help to build relationships and encourage responsibility in children.

How to find us

Write to us or phone the number below and you will be given details of your local contact:

Parent Network
Room 2, Winchester House
Kennington Park
11 Cranmer Road
London SW9 6EJ
Tel: 0171 735 1214

Of further interest...

The Secret of Happy Children

Steve Biddulph

The Secret of Happy Children helps you with parent-child communication from babyhood to teens. It has received widespread praise around the world as a book which gives you heart to be more yourself as a parent – stronger, more loving, more definite, more relaxed.

Steve Biddulph reveals what is really happening inside children's minds and what to do about it. You'll find yourself letting go of old, negative approaches, and freeing up more energy to enjoy your children and your life.

Steve Biddulph answers all of the questions he is most often asked:

- stopping tantrums before they start
- curing shyness in your children
- the skills of fathering
- how to cure whingeing kids
- being a single parent – how to make it easier
- kids and TV
- food and behaviour – it makes a huge difference
- the ten minutes that can save your marriage.

ISBN: 0 7225 3669 0
Price: £8.99

Available from Thorsons' 24 hour telephone ordering service on 0181 307 4052 or 0141 306 3349.

Manhood

Steve Biddulph

Most men don't have a life. So begins the most powerful, practical and honest book ever to be written about men and boys. Not about our problems – but about how we can find the joy and energy of being in a male body with a man's mind and spirit – about men's liberation.

Steve Biddulph, author of *Raising Boys* and the million-copy seller *The Secret of Happy Children*, writes about the turning point that men have reached – as reflected in films like The Full Monty. He gives practical, personal answers to how things can be different at home and work.

He tells powerful stories about healing the rift between fathers and sons. About friendship. How women and men can get along in dynamic harmonious ways. How boys can be raised to be healthy men.

Manhood has had a profound emotional impact on tens of thousands of readers worldwide, and has been passed from son to father, friend to friend, husband to wife, with the simple message 'you must read this!'

'Steve Biddulph should be in the UK what he is in Australia, the household name in the business of raising boys and being a man.' Dorothy Rowe

ISBN: 1 869890 99X

Price: £9.95

Publication date: 29 October 1998, available from Biblios, Star Road, Partridge Green, West Sussex RH13 8LD. Telephone: 01403 710851. Fax: 01403 711143.